Cartoons and Caricatures

The caricaturist used to be considered a scurrilous creature. In 1831, writing of Gillray's work, *The Athenaeum* said: 'The mere life of a caricaturist can neither be interesting nor instructive: for who would wish to know of the haunts and habits . . . of a spy . . . who insults inferiority of mind and exposes defects of body?' Yet, less than 150 years later, caricaturists are lauded, sometimes even knighted, while figures such as Grosz, Steinberg and Scarfe are counted by some among the great twentieth-century artists.

The cartoonist's skill did not receive much praise or attention until at the turn of the century the new science of psychology drew attention to its specific nature, spontaneity—a quality not previously over-valued in the world of art. Then, the works of artists such as Phil May, Phiz and Tenniel began to be appreciated. However, this previous neglect means that the cartoon has not been subjected to rigorous criticism or the fads and more corrosive nonsense of art movements; its aims—to satirize and entertain—have protected it. Fine art and applied art in one, it is well able to look after its own style and humour.

Bevis Hillier, *Harper's Bazaar*'s 'Antiques' columnist, has also written *The Turners of Lane End*, *Art Deco* and *Posters*. Here he gives us a lively survey of the art of caricature from the decorated documents of the thirteenth century to the strip cartoon of today.

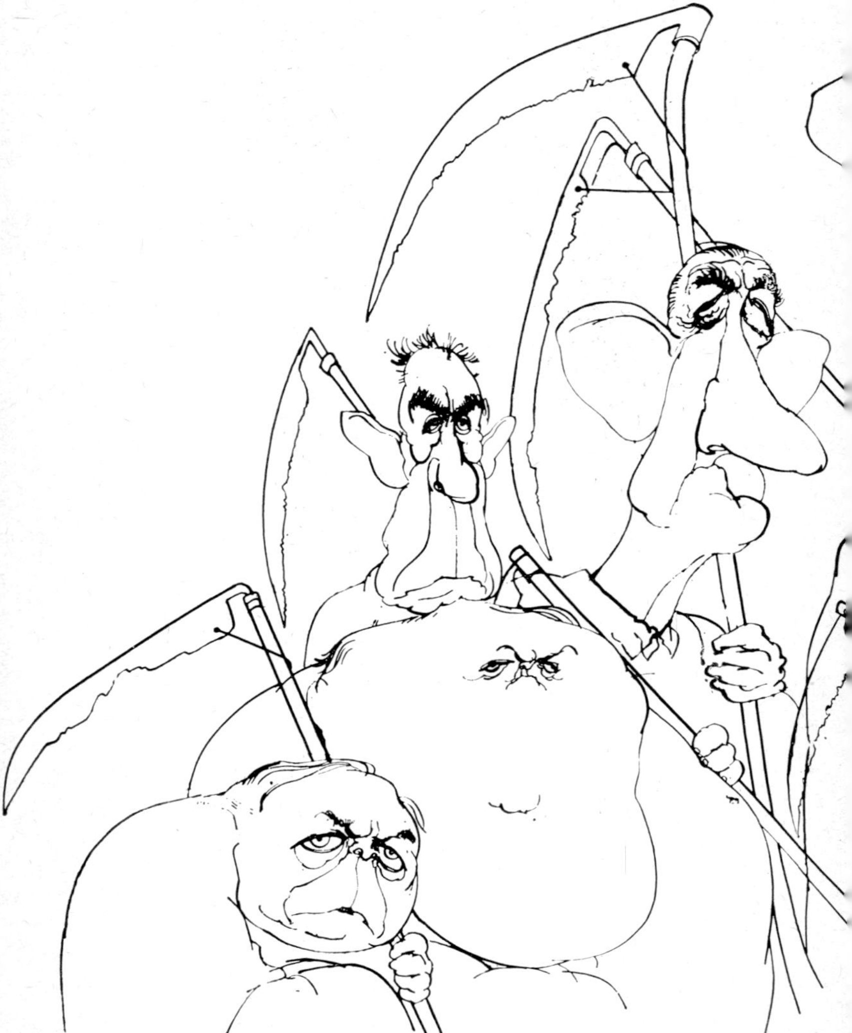

Cartoons and Caricatures

Bevis Hillier

General Editor David Herbert
Studio Vista/Dutton Pictureback

To Philip and Yvonne
Mansergh

and Natasha

© Bevis Hillier 1970
Published in London by Studio Vista Limited
Blue Star House, Highgate Hill, N19
and in New York by E. P. Dutton & Co. Inc.,
201 Park Avenue South, New York NY 10003
Set in 8D on 11 pt Univers 689
Made and Printed in Great Britain by
Richard Clay (The Chaucer Press) Ltd, Bungay, Suffolk
SBN 289 79694 6 (Paperback)
SBN 289 79695 4 (Hardback)

Contents

The Widow Ghooltooth.

Caricature by James Sullivan, c. 1885
Author's collection

Introduction

It is a modern trait to regard the more portentous art of the past as comic, and to take its caricatures seriously. W. F. Yeames's *Amy Robsart* which was bought in 1877 for the then huge sum of £1000, now languishes in the Tate Gallery vaults; but exhibitions are held of Phil May's spry sketches, which he used to give away in exchange for drinks. George Du Maurier, the Victorian cartoonist, lies under a simple wooden headboard in Hampstead churchyard, while Lord Leighton, the fêted President of the Royal Academy and the first English artist to be made a peer, rests under the bronze panoply of a tomb in St Paul's Cathedral; yet Mrs Leonée Ormond thinks that the book on Du Maurier which she has recently had published was just as worth writing as the biography of Leighton on which she and her husband are now engaged. The National Portrait Gallery, whose Director, in a letter to *The Times*, has bewailed the formal oil portraits by which he is surrounded—'the weary products of a tradition evolved in the Renaissance'—is as happy to hang a Max Beerbohm caricature of a man, as a society portrait by Sargent or de Laszlo.

The caricaturist used to be considered a scurrilous creature. In reviewing a life of Gillray in 1831, *The Athenaeum* said:

In caricatures, as in candles, there are wicks which will soon consume them; and the memories of the artists themselves may be safely permitted to perish with them. The mere life of a caricaturist can neither be interesting nor instructive: for who would wish to know of the haunts and habits of a sort of private and public spy . . . who insults inferiority of mind, and exposes defects of body— and who aggravates what is already hideous, and blackens what was before sufficiently dark.

Today, cartoonists are knighted; biographies of H. M. Bateman and 'Pont' have recently been published; caricaturists such as George Grosz, Saul Steinberg and Gerald Scarfe are counted by some among the great twentieth-century artists; the National Portrait Gallery recently held an exhibition of caricature.

What explains the new status of the caricature? Partly that, unlike academic painting, it represents the quality or essence of a person, not the person himself; what the artist felt as much as

Paper hat: nodding figure from a nineteenth-century game. 'Das komisch Parchen' (The comic couple) *James Reeve, Esq*

what he saw. Rather as Charlotte Brontë in *Villette* anticipated Freudian psychology without having formulated its principles, caricature contained the elements of twentieth-century art: distortion for effect; the avoidance of cloying lyricism and sentimentality, and of pedantic academicism; the idea that art should reflect one's own day; fragmentation (Cubism); frozen movement (Futurism); abstraction itself. Above all, it seemed 'unfinished',

8

possessing the quality of eloquent suggestion. Sir Joshua Reynolds, in his *Discourses to the Royal Academy*, gave an eighteenth-century view of why such sketches could appeal—a momentary defence of the unfinished which comes strangely from a man whose aim was to establish the dignity of art and the status of the artist, by great academies and grandiose history paintings:

It is true, sketches or such drawings as painters generally make for their works, give this pleasure of imagination to a high degree. From a slight undetermined drawing, where the ideas of the composition and character are, as I may say, only just touched upon, the imagination supplies more than the painter himself, probably, could produce; and we accordingly often find that the finished work disappoints the expectation that was raised from the sketch.

The sketches of which Reynolds was speaking were means, not ends: that is how they differ from caricatures, which, to adapt his phrase, are slight 'determined' drawings. Reynolds was not saying that the artist should aim for, or be content with, a lack of finish. He was merely observing that preliminary sketches could incidentally give scope for imaginative play—a kind of audience participation. The idea that an unfinished work could be as valid, even more valid, than a finished one, he would have thought preposterous. I am reminded of my teacher in the kindergarten, who, when she taught us how to fold a paper boat, said: 'Half-way to making the boat, you will find you have made a paper hat. Those who are not able to get any further, can put on the hat.' A paper hat is as amusing—or unamusing—as a paper boat; but because the latter was harder to make, it was a point of honour not to stop at the hat stage. The hat was regarded as a dunce's hat.

This parable seems to bear out Roger Fry's view that finish is something to be distrusted because it arises from non-aesthetic influences such as social ambition. He also felt that too much finish inhibited free artistic expression. Hitler's destruction of non-academic paintings encouraged the identification of fascism with finish. The other relevant twentieth-century development was the great informal science of psychology, which again suggested a way in which caricature might be thought superior to academic painting: the chance it gave for free and open expression of the artist's personality, not to mention that of his subject. The caricature was only one stage nearer formality than the 'doodle', the alleged seismograph of the unconscious.

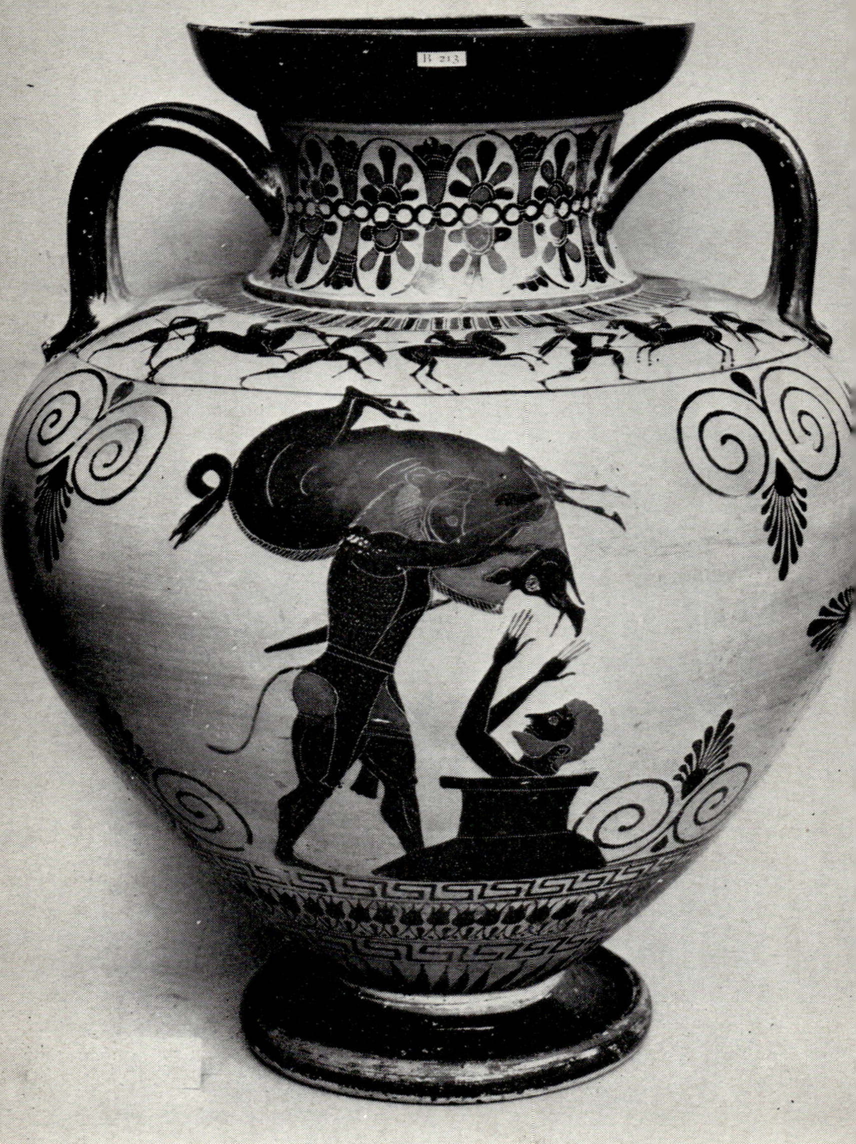
B 213

Early Secular Caricature

In a book of this size it is not possible to deal with the ancient incunabula of caricature, such as Greek vase paintings, the graffiti of Pompeii, or the great wealth of medieval wood carving, stone gargoyles and grotesques. The most elaborate of early ink caricatures—recognized by at least one writer as 'the earliest true caricature'—is in a vellum document of 1233 in the Public Record Office. It is an unofficial decoration at the head of a *Rotulus Judeorum*, presumably the work of an Exchequer clerk. The central figure is Isaac of Norwich, a wealthy Jew who owned a

Hercules bringing the boar to Eurystheus who has taken refuge in a storage jar. Attic black-figured jar found at Vulci; c. 540 B.C. *British Museum*

Gorgon's head; ornamental terracotta tile-end found at Ruvo but made at Tarentum, c. 520 B.C. *British Museum*

quay and considerable land in Norwich. He was the principal creditor of the abbot and monks of Westminster, who had the support of Pandulf, Bishop elect of Norwich and Papal Legate. Pandulf (whom Shakespeare made a main character in his *King John*) campaigned to have the Jews expelled from the country. Isaac is shown crowned, and has been given three faces; but probably as Luke Owen Pike suggests in his *History of Crime in England* (1873) a fourth face is to be understood, to indicate that Isaac is surveying his possessions, north, south, east and west. To the left is another Jew, Mosse Mokke, who was subsequently

Caricature of Isaac of Norwich and other Jews on a *Rotulus Judeorum* of 1233
Public Record Office

hanged for clipping coin. Below Isaac is a Jewess named Avegay. A horned devil has his finger on the nose of each. To the right is Dagon, god of Philistia, in a turret.

One of the grossest of early secular caricatures is a German woodcut of about 1510 which shows a toper with a belly so distended that it has to be carried before him in a wheelbarrow. The French pirated this objectionable figure for a broadsheet of 1635 to satirize General Matthias Galas (1584–1647), the victorious commander of the Austrian army during the wars in the Netherlands.

Indeed, it is in the early seventeenth century that caricatures of foreign enemies first become common. If you could not show your enemy as a coward, you could at least show him as a dwarf or a braggart: the two types are well shown in a German engraving of a papal Swiss guard, and in *Captain Fracasse* by Callot's friend

Papal Swiss Guard: German caricature of the sixteenth century

The toper: a German wood engraving of 1510

Pantaleon Bürgman auf der Wacht von der
Schweitzer Guarde zu Rom.

Das alte Pantle Gschlecht ist allewil tapfer gsi,
Halt wie a Bidermah, trapt mini hungerst
Gos frisß, wen ma zu Feld da trimma Kuhl ruhrt
Wie gimpf mirs Herß im Lib bis daß ma cumadrs
Do nimb iß schned schuß her schlag kirtel a hir
Zill neaba da Kuhl durts, laß zirußa auff mir Mahn

15

Abraham Bosse (1602–76), a portrait of a strutting lout who symbolizes the boorish arrogance of Spanish and Italian officers. But as the carnage mounted in the Thirty Years War, all the combatant countries began to realize how socially destructive and futile war could be. There were German caricatures of the *Soldatenmangel*— a cruel Leviathan stuffs one man into his fanged mouth while grabbing for more victims with his other claw. In Ausgburg a print entitled *Bellum Symbolicum* appeared: an armour-plated monster breathes fire at a terrified fop in slashed silk. On a higher plane of art, Callot depicted the horrors of war with a flaying ferocity that would not be rivalled until Goya's series *Los Desastros de la Guerra*.

'Captain Fracasse', engraving by **Abraham Bosse** (1602–76)

The Reformation

Satire was mobilized by the invention of printing in the fifteenth century; and by the time of the Reformation the age of book illustration had begun. Caricature was used as a weapon by both Reformers and counter-Reformers. Luther's friend Lucas Cranach illustrated a book by Philip Melancthon, *The Passionale of Christ and Antichrist*, in 1521, contrasting by facing woodcuts the simplicity of Christ's life with the luxurious pomp of the Pope's: Christ washing the disciples' feet while an emperor kisses the

The 'monk-calf of Freiberg'. German wood engraving, first half of sixteenth century

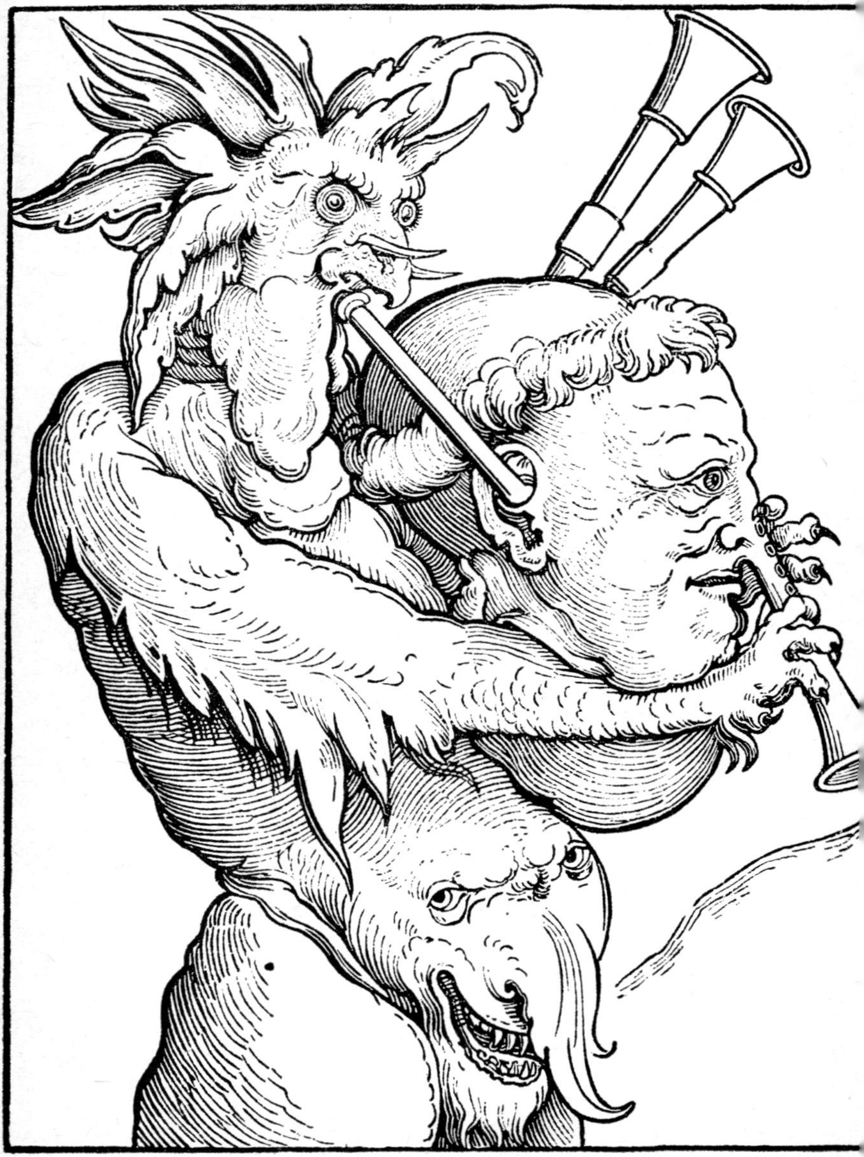

Pope's toe; Christ refusing earthly dignities while the Pope is surrounded by cardinals and bishops, warriors and fortifications; Christ in thorns, the Pope enthroned in worldly glory; and so on. The final pair of illustrations juxtapose the Ascension of Christ and the consignment of the Pope to hellfire by enthusiastic demons. The hatred of the Papacy expressed in a woodcut illustration to a pamphlet by Luther and Melancthon of the *Pope-Donkey of Rome* was matched by the satire of monastic corruption in another chimera, the *Monk-Calf of Freiberg*.

The anti-Luther caricatures were on about the same level. One woodcut shows a devil playing bagpipes formed of Luther's head. It is dated 1521 and commemorates Luther's examination before the Diet of Worms.

Martin Luther as the Devil's bagpipes. German wood engraving, first half of sixteenth century

Great artists as caricaturists

Many would consider Leonardo da Vinci (1452–1519) the greatest of all caricaturists. His grotesque heads with nutcracker jaws, squat noses, simian upper lips, cataracts of chins and eyes swimming in rheum are like the permutations of some infernal identikit game invented by demons for a god to play with. But the fact that in one drawing of a hideous old man his profile is parodied in the folds at the back of his neck seems to support Professor Gombrich's view in his King Penguin on caricature (1940) : 'a closer examination . . . shows that they are rather an artist's experiment in various forms of ugliness and expression than portraits of individuals'.

Gian Lorenzo Bernini (1598–1680) : caricature of a cardinal (Scipio Borghese ?) *Vatican Library, Rome*

Annibale Carracci (1560–1609), known mainly as an exponent of the 'grand manner', indulged in caricature when he relaxed from the loftiness of his academic style. The quest for perfect form was temporarily abandoned in search of the perfect deformity. A caricature by him of an Italian singer and his wife is in the National Museum, Stockholm. He is said to have portrayed his friends as animals. Gian Lorenzo Bernini (1598–1680), the apocalyptic master of the baroque, could similarly leave his poniarded saints and ecstasiated virgins to scrawl a caricature of a cardinal, his lips clamped shut in an expression of dogmatic complacency. Bernini may have introduced Pier Leone Ghezzi (1674–1755) to caricature. Ghezzi was able to make a living out of portrait caricature. His head of the organist and composer Pergolese (dated 1734) is characteristic of his loose but expressive technique. A drawing

Pier Leone Ghezzi (1674–1755) : caricature of the musician Pergolese, 1734

Jacques Callot (1593 ?–1635) : caricature of Philippe Thomassin and his wife, 1611

Giovanni Batista Tiepolo (1696–1770) : caprice drawing

attributed to him, in the Kupferstichkabinett der Akademie der Bildenden Künste, Vienna, shows an emaciated artist entertaining fat, bemedalled patrons in his studio.

One of the minor skirmishes of nineteenth-century art history was the recurrent debate as to whether the elder Brueghel or Rabelais himself had drawn the weird grotesques which were published in Paris in 1565 as illustrations to the *Songes Drôlatiques de Pantagruel*. Paul Lacroix believed that Rabelais was the artist. Champfleury thought they were by Brueghel. The argument, which was still alive in 1926 when Bohun Lynch published his *History of Caricature*, turned on the precise interpretation of a Latin sentence written by Rabelais to Cardinal du Bellay in 1534.

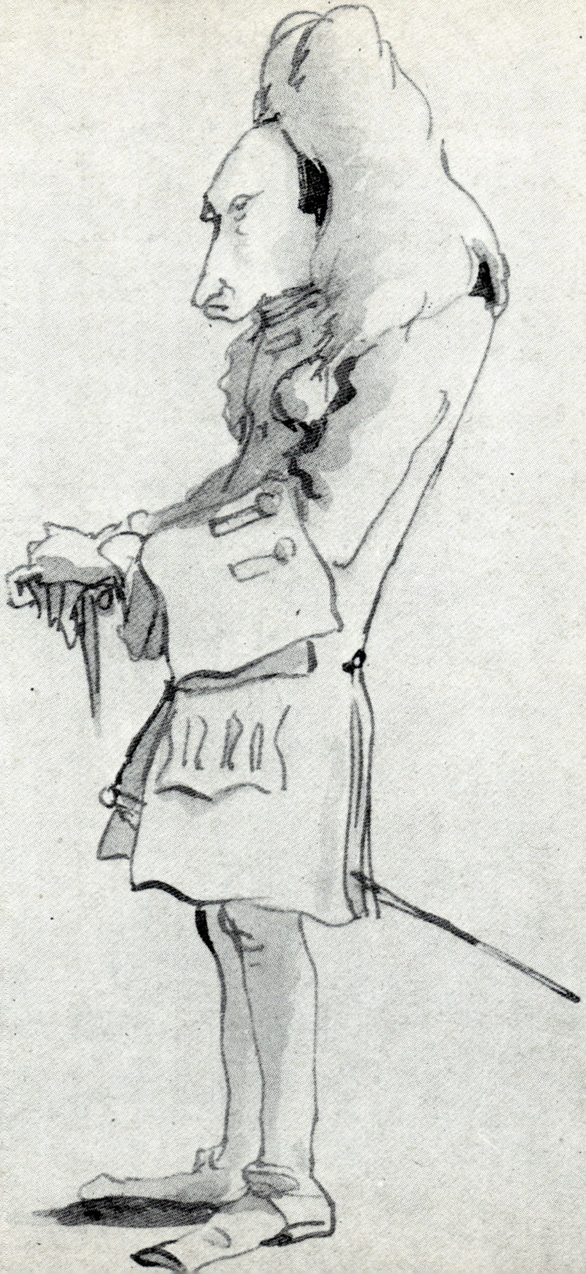

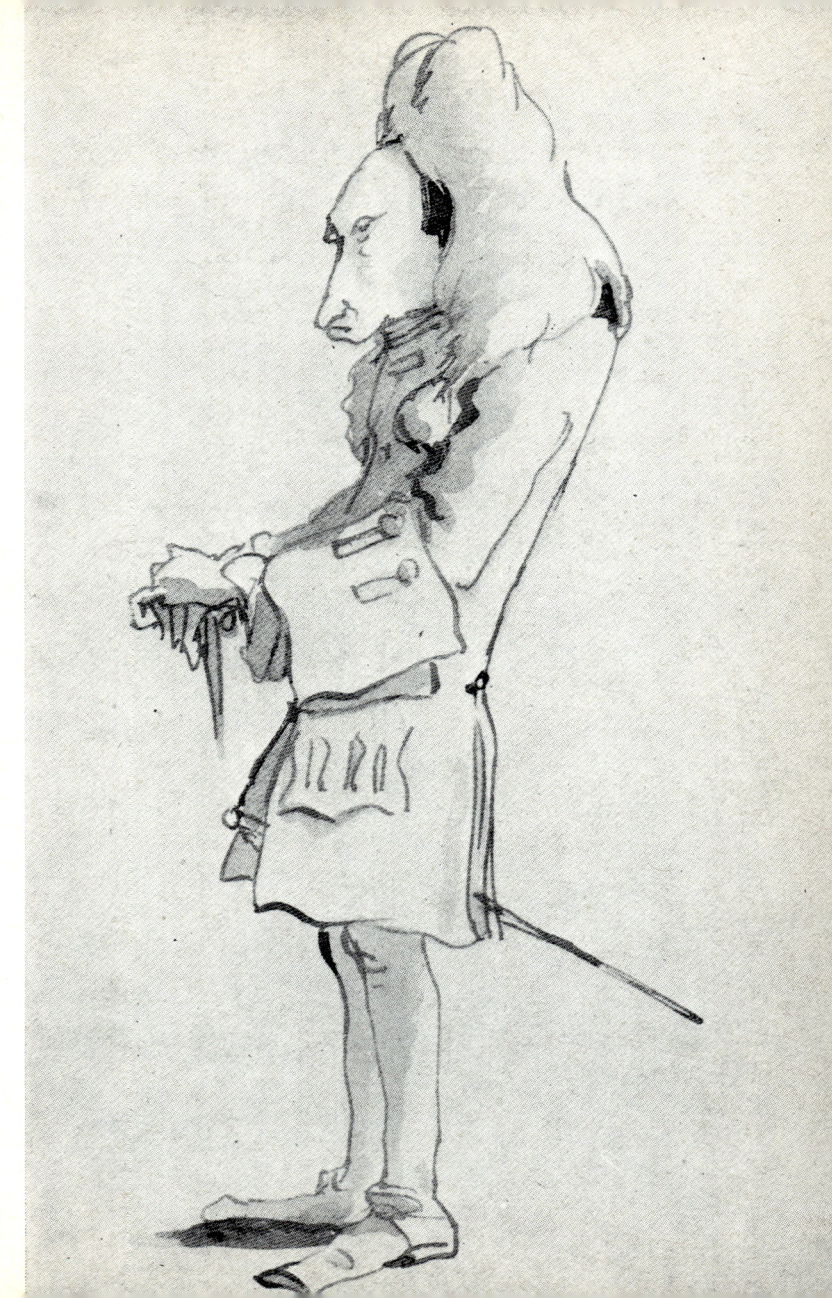

It is now generally agreed that the actual artist was François Desprez; but his woodcuts were certainly inspired by Rabelais's text and he was probably influenced by prints of Brueghel's work —so neither of the disputants was entirely wrong.

The *Caprices* of Jacques Callot (1593?–1635) are more calligraphic and nervously drawn. He was also capable of impromptu caricatures of personal acquaintances. When he left Florence for Rome in 1611, after a quarrel with his master, the engraver Philippe Thomassin (with whose wife he had allegedly had an affair), he caricatured Thomassin as an Italian Comedy figure, giving the engraver's wife the snout of a pig.

François Desprez: illustrations to the *Songes Drôlatiques de Pantagruel*, 1565

There is a similar informality in the *Caprices* with which Giovanni Batista Tiepolo (1696–1770) occupied his leisure in eighteenth-century Venice. A selection of them has been published with an introduction by a modern cartoonist, Mr Osbert Lancaster. Of the *Caprices* he observes: 'Here he is not concerned with the greater glory of Prince–Bishops or Most Catholic Majesties; there is no need now for him to simulate a religious ecstasy he was incapable of experiencing; he is free to work for his own pleasure and enjoyment'. These little drawings of skeletal aristocrats, jovial servants and lightermen, are just the kind of thing the English milord brought home with him as a souvenir; they certainly had an

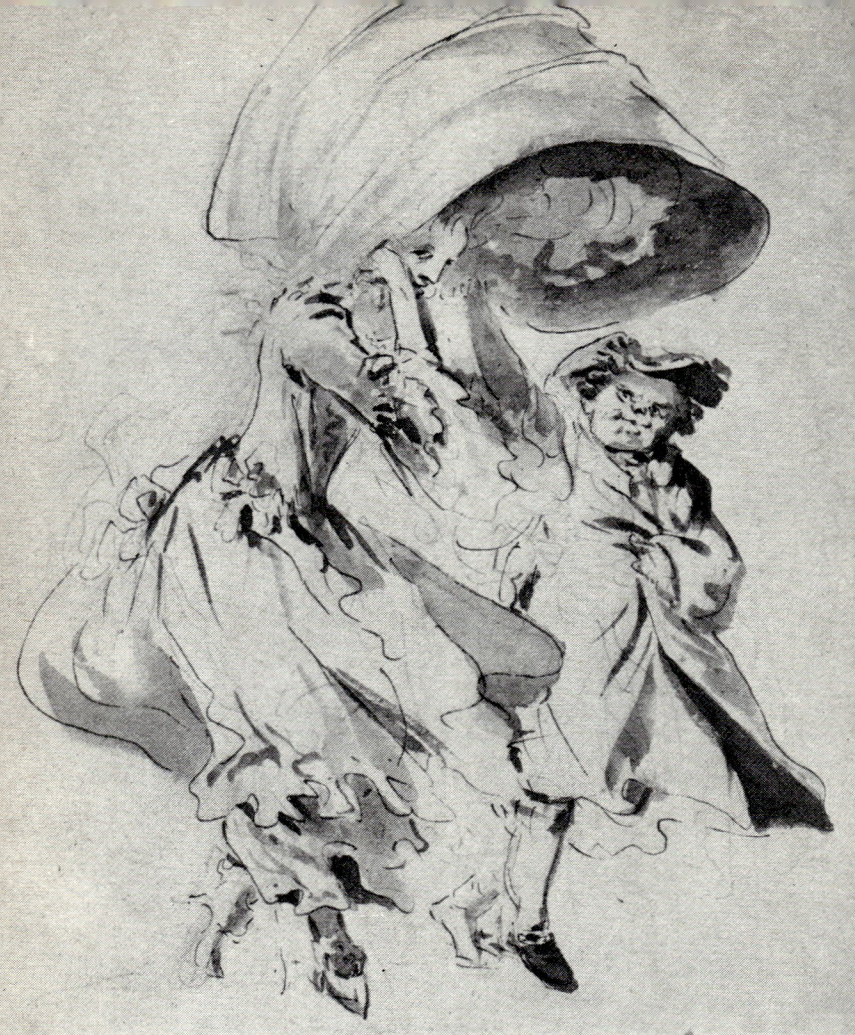

Elias Martin (1739–1818) : caricature of Johan Fredrik Martin and his wife
National Museum, Stockholm

effect on the style of Thomas Patch, and may have influenced
Rowlandson and Gillray too.

Sweden produced three extraordinarily talented caricaturists
in the eighteenth century. Elias Martin (1739–1818), Johan

Johan Tobias Sergel (1740–1814) : caricature of J. H. Fuseli, c 1775
National Museum, Stockholm

Tobias Sergel (1740–1814) and Admiral Count Carl August Ehrensvärd (1745–1800) were all born in Stockholm. None would have considered himself primarily a caricaturist : caricature was a desultory relaxation from the noble neo-classical painting by

Carl August Ehrensvärd, 'My Friend shall Drink and be voluptuously drowned' dated 1797 *National Museum, Stockholm*

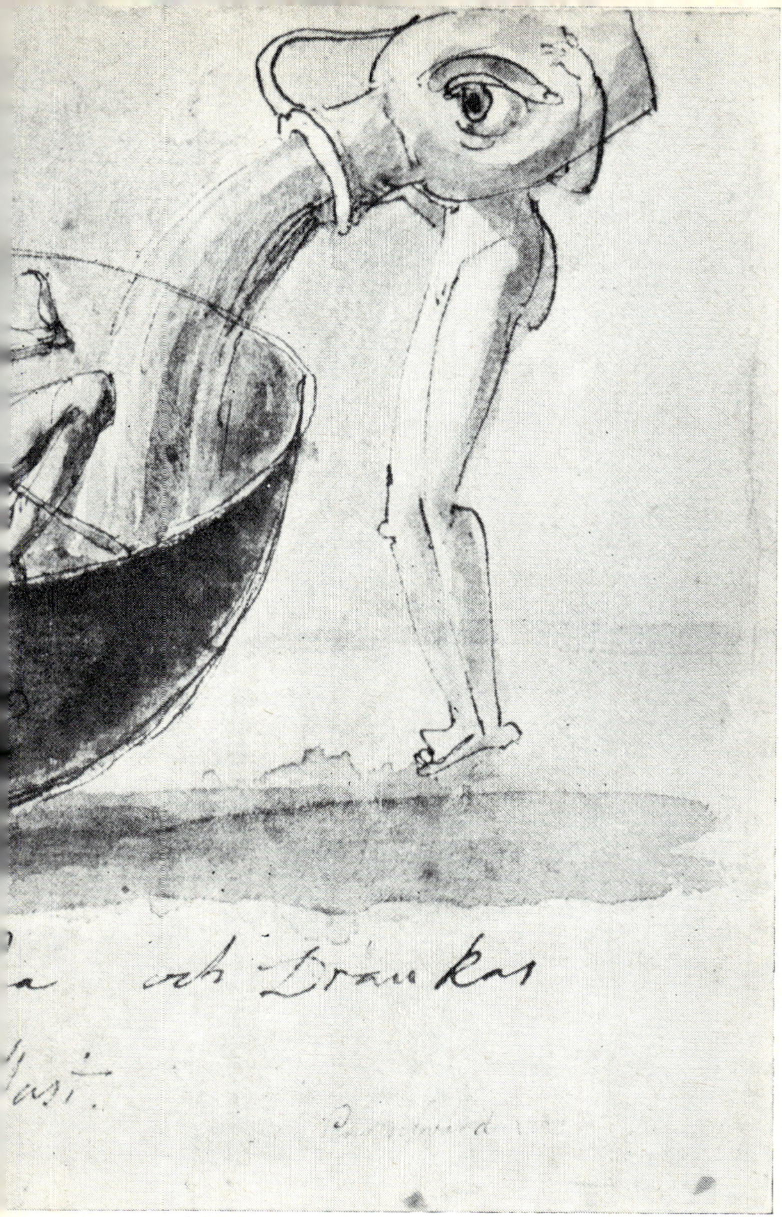
a och Dränkas

Carl August Ehrensvärd (1745–1800): 'The Real Birth of the Poet', dated 1795 *National Museum, Stockholm*

which they really set store. Yet Martin's sketch of his hunchback brother Johan Fredrik and his wife, Sergel's grotesque of the Swiss painter Fuseli (in front of St Peter's, Rome) and Ehrensvärd's strange erotic-surrealist drawings of the *Poet's Birth* and the 'voluptuous drowning' of a friend show something of the genius of a group of artists whose work is not widely enough known.

Great Britain: Hogarth to 'Max'

Caricature came to England from Italy as an aristocratic diversion, a cliquish joke. As such it did not appeal to William Hogarth, who saw in it an intrusion of the amateur into what he was trying to make the profession of artist; an attack on Nature and a denial of draughtsmanship. When he etched and engraved *The Bench* in 1758, with its portraits of Sir John Willes and the sleeping Lord Bathurst, he ironically dedicated it to George, later Marquis Townshend (1724–1807—who became Lord Lieutenant of Ireland) the leading amateur caricaturist in England. In the fourth

H. W. Bunbury, The Gaming Table. Late eighteenth century
The Fine Art Society, Ltd

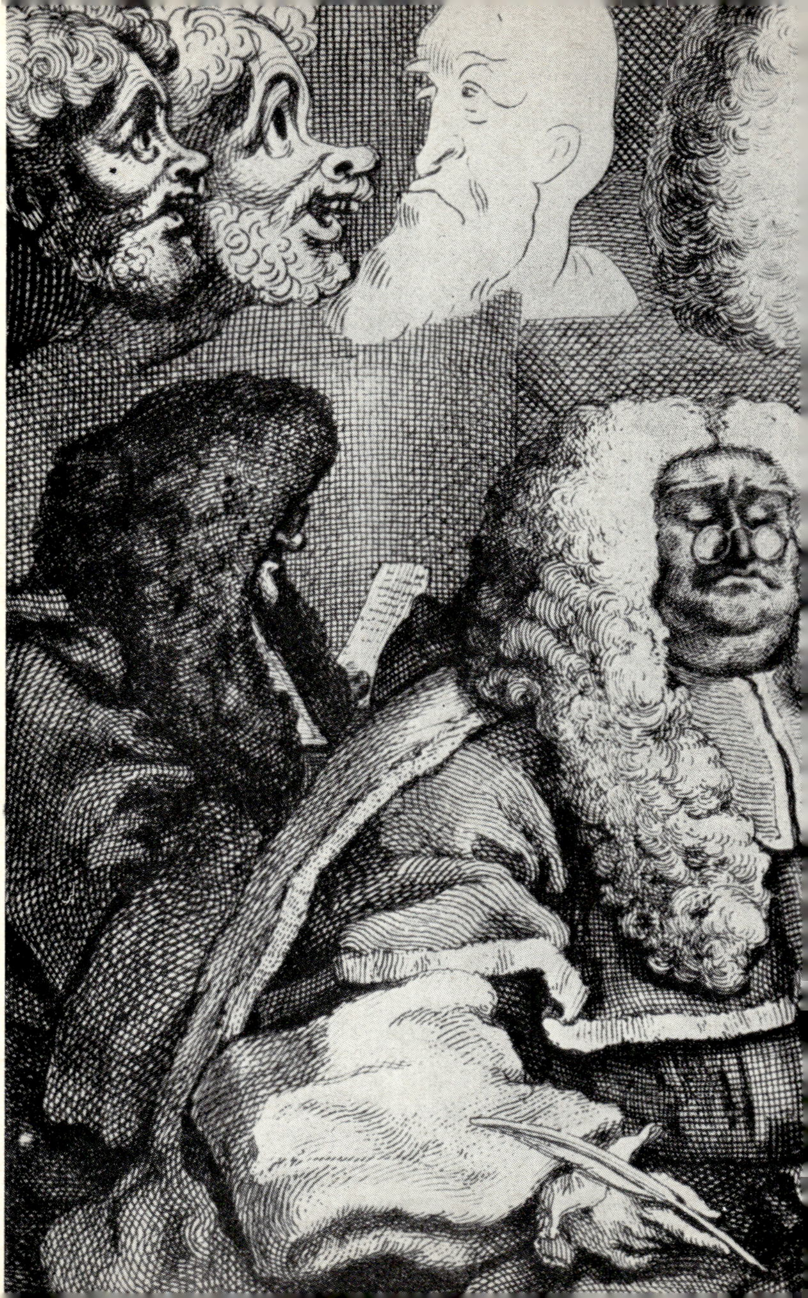

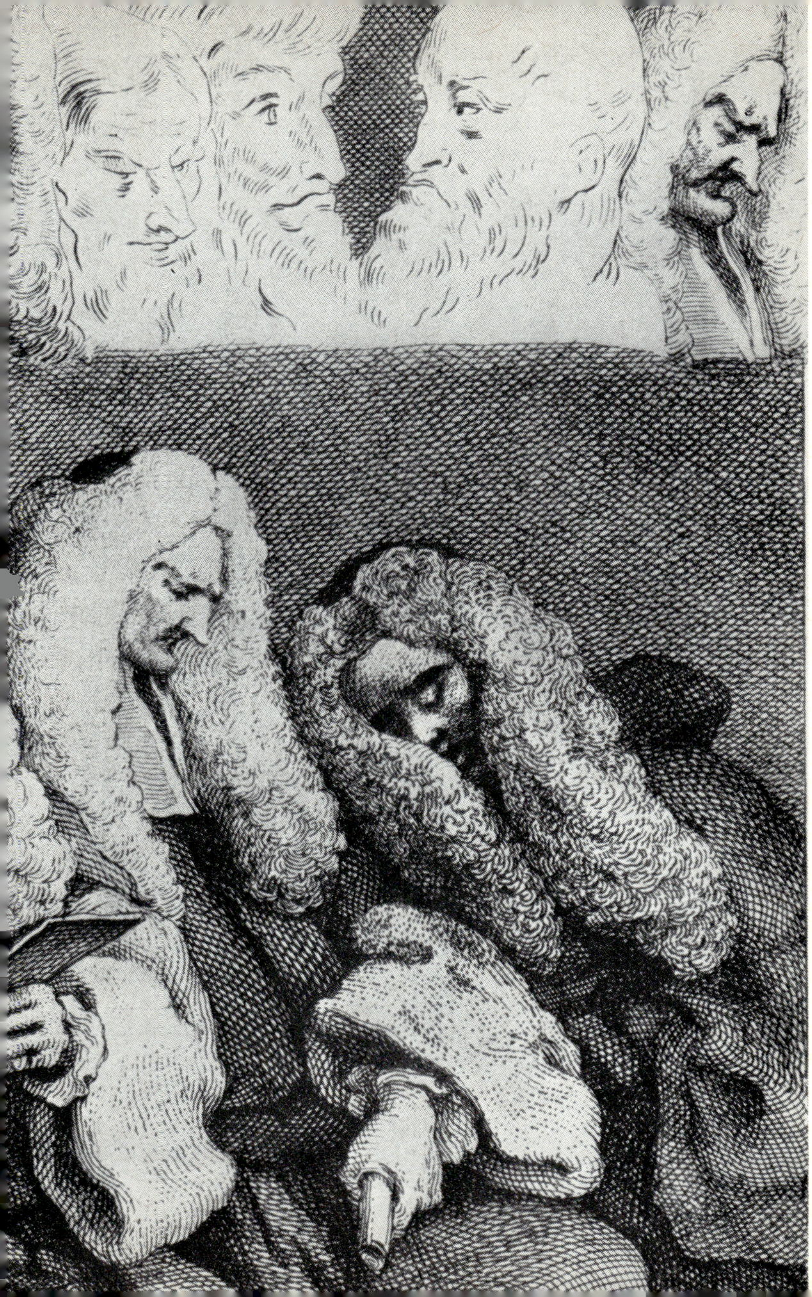

state of the etching-engraving, he added at the top two profiles of the Lame Man in Raphael's *Sacrifice of Lystra* and a group of heads from Leonardo's *Last Supper*, separated by two versions of his sleeping judge: to show how drawing deteriorates the more it diverges from Nature. In the *Analysis of Beauty* he wrote:

Now that which has of late years got the name of *Caracatura*, is, or ought to be, totally divested of every stroke that hath a tendency to good drawing: it may be said to be a species of lines that are produc'd rather by the hand of chance than of skill . . . I remember a famous *Caracatura* of a certain Italian singer, that struck at first sight, which consisted only of a straight perpendicular stroke with a dot over it.

To hear Hogarth, whom we are bound to think one of the greatest English caricaturists, inveighing against caricature, is extraordinary; but it was Hogarth who converted caricature from a fashionable divertissement into an art form and an expression of the age. *The Rake's Progress* and *Marriage-à-la-Mode* are caricature on the highest level. And by applying the same formidable technique to slum subjects like *Gin Lane*, Hogarth proved that caricature (though he would not have used the term) did not have to be a fribbling art by aristocrats, of aristocrats, for aristocrats.

Caricature persisted as an upper class hobby throughout the eighteenth century, but it also attracted humbler men such as Matthew Darley, who was an artists' colourman with a shop in the Strand. He was an engraver (Anthony Pasquin was apprenticed to him to learn the art) and a publisher (he published some of Henry Bunbury's early sketches) but is best known as a caricaturist. Altogether he produced some three hundred caricatures, including the splendid conceit of the *grande dame's* coiffure garnished with flowerbeds, and in 1778 he advertised a 'comic exhibition'.

Henry William Bunbury (1750–1811) came, on the other hand, from an ancient Norman family which in Stephen's time was established at Bunbury in Cheshire. He was the second son of the Rev. Sir William Bunbury, Bart., of Mildenhall, Suffolk. Educated at Westminster and Cambridge, he showed great precocity: at school he etched *A Boy riding on a Pig*, a copy of which is in the British Museum, and at Cambridge he collected a gallery of ridiculous dons. In 1771 he married Catherine Horneck, to whom Goldsmith addressed his 'Letter in Verse and Prose' two years later. Bunbury (surely Wilde must have borrowed the absurd name

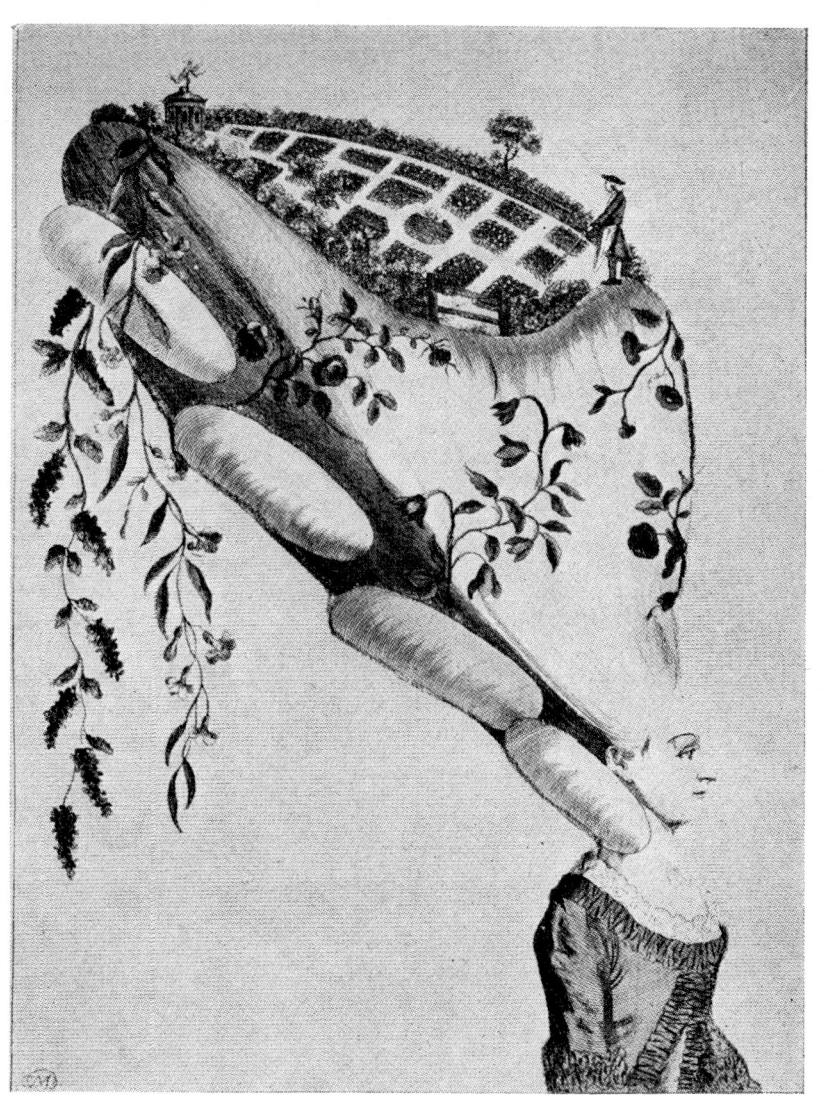

Matthew Darley: 'The Flower Garden', 1777

from him for the mythical invalid in *The Importance of Being Ernest?*) was a friend of Goldsmith, Garrick and Reynolds, and a favourite of the Duke and Duchess of York, to whom he was appointed equerry in 1787. He made the Grand Tour in France and Italy and studied drawing in Rome—although one would hardly guess it from the bucolic crudity of his pictorial style. His talent was well suited to illustrating *Tristram Shandy*, or to drawing the thunderous figure of Dr Johnson, who appears in his print of 1781, *A Chop House*.

If Bunbury, with all his chances to see the masterpieces of Italian art, never rose much above a rough-and-ready hacks' style, we cannot expect from contemporary self-made caricaturists more than a tempered primitivism. John Kay and 'Tim Bobbin' were both primitives, in that their style had that simple, mystic, John Clare quality which comes of self-education within limited horizons, yet both were capable of greater subtlety than Bunbury.

John Kay was born near Dalkieth in 1742, and at the age of thirteen was apprenticed to a barber there. He remained there for six years, and spent a further seven years as a journeyman barber in Edinburgh. In 1771 he purchased the freedom of the city and was enrolled as a member of the Society of Surgeon-Barbers. He set up in business on his own, and devoted his spare time to portrait caricature. He found a patron in William Nisbet of Dirleton; Nisbet died in 1784 and his heir settled £20 a year on Kay. In 1785 Kay retired and took up caricature fulltime, the earliest of his dated etchings being a self-portrait, inscribed 1786. He sold his etchings from a little shop in Edinburgh. He etched nearly nine hundred plates, of almost every notable Scotsman of his time, except for Burns. His etchings of Adam Smith are, with the posthumous medallions by Tassie, the only authentic likenesses. Kay died in 1826.

John Collier was more than thirty years older than Kay, yet the difference between their satires is often so little that one could imagine the drawings to be the work of the same man. Collier was born in 1708 at Urmston, near Manchester, the son of a parson-schoolmaster. His father lost his sight and was therefore unable to fulfil his original purpose of training John for the church. Instead,

John Collier, Self-portrait engraving: 1773

Within the oval frame: TIM · BOBBIN ·

On the open book and papers: Lancashire Dialect · Remarks Histor.ᵗ Lanche ller

37

Collier's illustration to his poem 'The Battle of the Flying Dragon', 1777

Thomas Rowlandson: the fruitgirl and the dons *The Fine Art Society, Ltd*

Thomas Gillray: 'The March to the Bank', 1787

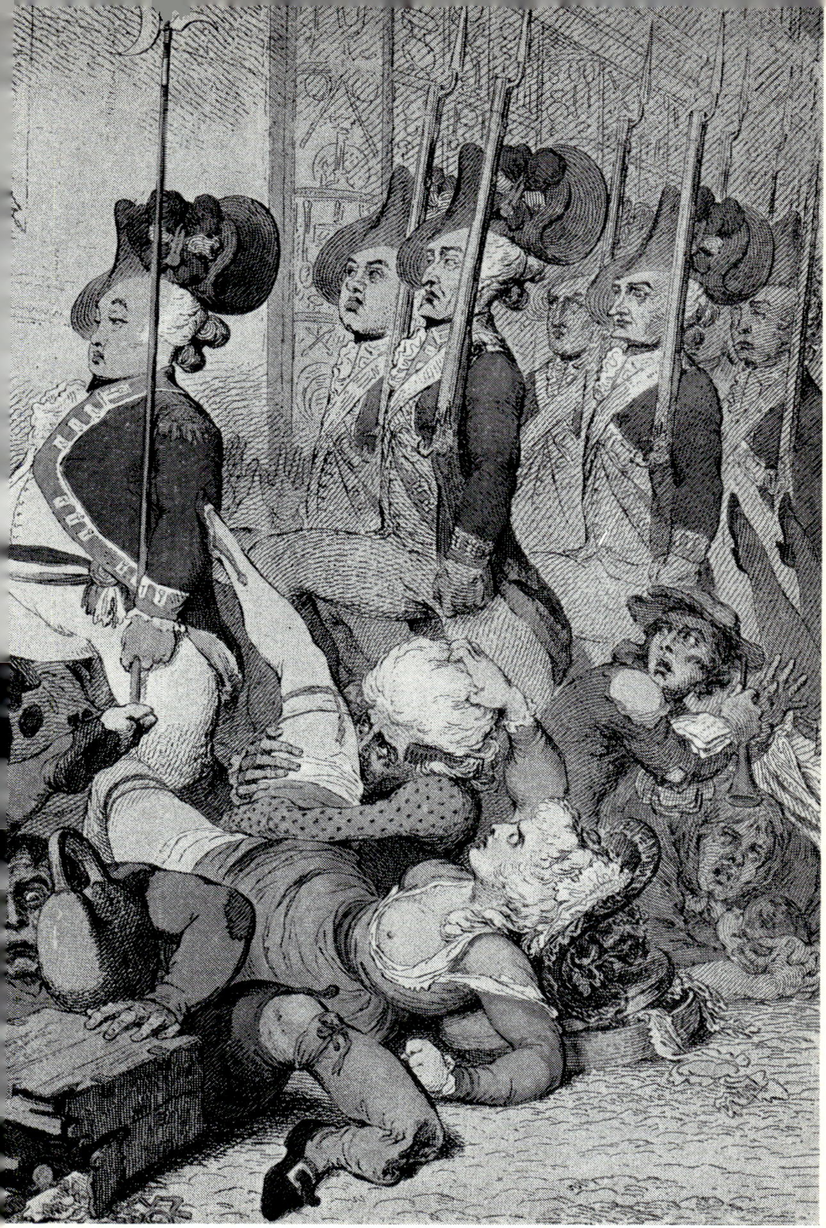

George Cruikshank, decorated signature of 1858 *Author's Collection*

Collier was apprenticed to a dutch-loom weaver in 1722. He had no taste for such handicraft and became an itinerant schoolmaster instead. In his free time he taught drawing and played on the hautboy and flute. He was considered quite a buck locally, and when once he wore some girls' paste pearls to church he set a fashion followed by other young men of the district. In 1740 he published a satire on a Lancashire Justice, *The Blackbird*. He married in 1744 a young lady of fashion, who brought with her a dowry of £300, which Collier seems to have spent largely on drink. He painted signs for innkeepers, and then, to make money, took to portrait caricature. His fame spread to Liverpool, and some of the merchants there bought his works for export to the West Indies and America. But his main ambition was to produce something literary that would survive him. This was his *View of the Lancashire Dialect; containing the Adventures and Misfortunes of a Lancashire Clown: by Tim Bobbin*. In this he published the dialects of the places he had visited in the years of travel. The book soon went into second and third editions. One of his patrons, Richard Hill, took him on as a counting clerk in his manufacture of baizes and shalloons; but soon found that 'a man might be a very pleasant companion over a bottle, yet be neither so useful nor expeditious at the ledger as an individual of sober habits'. Collier went back to his school. He died at Milnrow in 1786. His biographer, John Corry, expressed in 1862 an honest, not condescending, view of his achievement: 'His poetical flights . . . never rise higher than those of a moor cock on Blackstonedge.' His illustrations to his own bawdy verses *The Battle of the Flying Dragon* (which in fact concerns an errant pig-tail) are characteristically genial and vulgar.

Collier and Kay are backwater figures of British caricature. The mainstream, after Hogarth, is represented by Rowlandson and Gillray. Thomas Rowlandson (1756–1827) had a triumphant facility in line, movement and composition, the very reverse of the staid little scenes, peopled by stiffly articulated marionettes, that Collier and Kay produced. Like Hogarth, Rowlandson is primarily a social satirist. He has the same memory for significant detail, and the same adaptability in transferring his mockery from one social group to another. He might almost be the ideal pupil for whom Hogarth's *Analysis of Beauty* was written, with all the 'serpentine lines', 'tender tints' and lack of academy brown that Hogarth had recommended. But Rowlandson is less 'tough' an artist than Hogarth: altogether more frivolous, flirtatious and rococo. The two can be directly compared, since Rowlandson made a copy of Hogarth's *Shrimp Girl* (the former is at Windsor, the latter in the National Gallery.) Rowlandson has converted the charming natural smile of Hogarth's girl into a Bath pumproom simper; her rude good health into a boudoir complexion; her smock into an elegant gown; even her hat ribbon has been prettified into new frills and bows. No one could accuse Rowlandson of a Greuse-type sentimentality; but even his broadest humour, such as the

November the Ninth.
Grand Chorus of Aldermen.

The Guy
Please to ...
The Ninth

John Leech (1817–64) 'The Guy Mayor's Day—November the Ninth'
44

Day.

A new Lord Mayor we have got {We know no reason, When Fiddles in season,} Why dinner should be for

Allan Cuthbertson, Esq.

45

Exhibition Stare-case, is given a rosy, refined eroticism more French than English.

Gillray, by contrast, does not mince his lines. To him a *sans-culotte* is a man without trousers. Perhaps because of the repressiveness of his childhood among the death-welcoming Moravian sect in Chelsea, the sexual escapades in his caricatures are more enthusiastically explicit than Rowlandson's. The men grappling with the (literally) fallen women in *The March to the Bank* (1787) are taking greater liberties than any in the *Exhibition Stare-case*. And Gillray, unlike Rowlandson, is primarily a political caricaturist. The artist satirizing the drolleries of a country market is likely to show less *saeva indignatio* than one with a corrupt politician in his sights. Gillray was unsparing. In a splendid mixed metaphor, *The Athenaeum* of 1831 said of him: 'He did not seek to conceal his poisonous draughts in a gilded cup. He lived like a caterpillar on the green leaf of reputation.' Gillray's lean and lathy Pitt, with the turn-up nose and grasshopper legs, his bloated blotchy Sheridan, and scowling, unshaven Fox were caricature archetypes. We encounter the same sunken-cheeked or puffy creatures in the nineteenth-century engravings of George Cruikshank: Boney is just the regalvanized skeleton of Pitt. It was the venom and popularity of Gillray's prints that first made politicians realize the importance of caricature as a party-political propaganda weapon. A previous generation of politicians had had their tame poets: the Tories had Pope, while the Whigs could only recruit Edward Young:

> My breast, O Walpole, glows with grateful fire.
> The streams of royal bounty, turn'd by thee,
> Refresh the dry domains of poesy.

Now it was time to conscribe the artists. Gillray, like *Private Eye* today, was fairly impartial in his attacks; but his chief rival, James Sayers (1748–1823) was rewarded by a marshalship of the Exchequer Court in 1786 for his servile support of Pitt. The first knighthoods for caricaturists were Tenniel's (1893) and Francis Carruthers Gould's (1906). Rosebery once described Gould as 'one of the few remaining assets of the [Liberal] party'.

On this system, Gillray should have been given a peerage for his anti-Bonaparte propaganda during the Napoleonic wars. So should George Cruikshank. Gillray was now at the zenith of his popularity. In 1802 an *émigré*, having stood outside Gillray's publisher's window, wrote: 'The enthusiasm is indescribable when the next drawing appears; it is a veritable madness. You have to make your way in through the crowd with your fists.' Gillray's and Cruikshank's anti-Bonaparte caricatures were also disseminated by transfer-prints on jugs and mugs produced in the Staffordshire potteries. In ale-houses and country kitchens the caricatures of spindleshanked Boneys being humiliated by decent, ruddy John Bulls acted as a morale-booster; in 1943 Thomas Rosner produced a book setting Churchill's wartime speeches alongside Cruikshank's Bonaparte satires. He called it *The Writing on the Wall*.

George Cruikshank (1792–1878) was the son of Isaac Cruikshank (1756?–1811), a not very talented caricaturist whose reputation has lately been unduly inflated by the publication of two (nevertheless excellent) books: a *catalogue raisonné* of his works by Dr E. B. Krumbhaar (1967) and an edition by Robert Wark of his newly-discovered *Drawings for Drolls* (1968). A well-meaning

Sir John Tenniel (1820–1914): cartoon of Gladstone and John Bright *From a print taken from the original wood-block in the author's possession, on* The Times *press at Printing House Square*

Too ~~[illegible]~~ windy for Straws
just now;

Yours ever,

The Man who caught

at

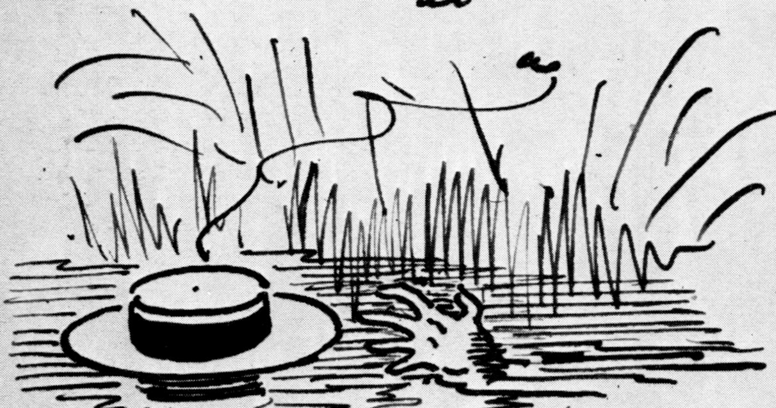
a

Nov. 7th. 1890

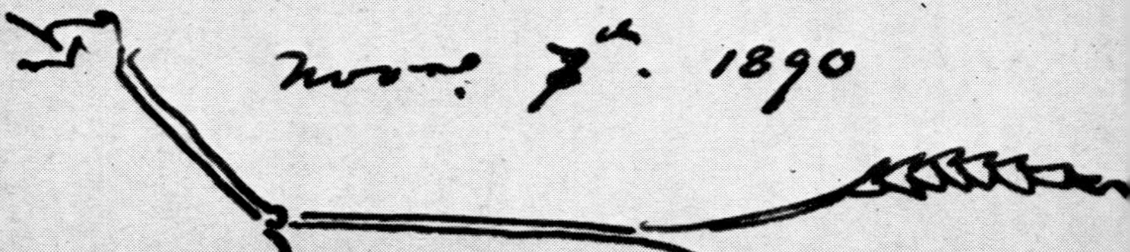

old lady is said to have asked Canova's son, 'And do you intend to go into your father's business?' The question would not have been quite so tactless applied to George Cruikshank. He and his brother Robert must count as the first hereditary caricaturists.

Apart from his Bonaparte works, he satirized Joanna Southcott and her Box, the corn laws and property tax, the purchase of the Elgin marbles, Princess Charlotte's marriage and the quarrels of the Regent and his wife. To William Hone's *Everyday Book* he contributed what he considered the 'great event of his artistic life': the *Bank Restriction Note* of 1818. Horrified by the sight of several women dangling from the gallows at Newgate for uttering forged pound notes, he designed, with lavish decoration of fetters and figures pendant, a 'Bank-note—not to be Imitated'. Hone made £700 from this stunt, and no person was ever afterwards hung for passing forged pound notes. When Peel finally revised the penal

Opposite and below:
Edward Linley Sambourne (1844–1910): decorated letter and envelope, 1890 *Author's collection*

code, Cruikshank claimed, without overwhelming modesty, that 'the final effect of my note was to stop the hanging for all minor offences'. As a teetotaller, Cruikshank also published several caricatures illustrating the horrible effects of alcohol. In this crusade he was less successful.

While Cruikshank was engaged in these public causes, the old elementary portrait caricature—figure and physiognomy—was being continued in a sophisticated form by Robert Dighton (1752?–1814). Dighton was not ambitious, but what he set out to do, he achieved perfectly. His caricatures of dandies and dons, usually in exact profile, evoke, as vividly as Captain Gronow's memoirs, the England of Byron with its fashionable clubs, 'quizes', disastrous gambling and dissipated colleges. Dighton himself entered into the immorality of the age. In 1806 it was discovered that he had stolen from the British Museum a number of etchings and prints. The Trustees met to consider the outrage on 21 June. Dighton had first visited the museum in 1794 and had gained the friendship and confidence of an obliging official by drawing his portrait and that of his daughter. Prints were lightly pasted in guard-books from which Dighton removed them unobserved and carried them off in a portfolio, sometimes substituting copies. A dealer named Woodburn gave evidence to the Trustees that he had bought a Rembrandt etching from Dighton. The latter confessed, but was not prosecuted.

A number of caricature magazines flourished in the early nineteenth century. Between 1811 and 1815, Cruikshank contributed to *The Scourge*, edited by Jack Mitford, a sailor who had served under Nelson, and to *The Satirist; or Monthly Meteor*. Mitford also edited *The Bon Ton* magazine and *The Quizzical Gazette*. Robert Seymour, who suggested to Dickens the idea of the *Pickwick Papers*, and illustrated them until he committed suicide in 1836, drew a series of political and social caricatures called *The Looking Glass* and also contributed to Gilbert A'Beckett's periodical *Figaro in London*. *Punch*, or *The London Charivari*, named after Charles Philipon's French magazine, was founded in 1841, and ruled over English caricature until the appearance of *Private Eye* in the early 1960s. At the outset, its leading caricaturist was John Leech (1817–64), who in his career on the magazine earned £40,000 and executed some 3000 drawings. He was born in London, the son of the proprietor of the London coffee-house on

Ludgate Hill. He was educated at Charterhouse, where he formed a friendship with Thackeray. At sixteen he began to study medicine at St Bartholomew's, but when his father's fortunes collapsed, he had to give up medicine, and he turned to art for a living. His best known cartoon is of Lord John Russell chalking up 'No Popery' on Cardinal Wiseman's door and running away (a reference to the 'Papal aggression' disputes). Leech indeed gave the word 'cartoon' its present meaning, for when an exhibition was held of cartoons for frescoes to decorate the new Houses of Parliament, he parodied them in six 'cartoons'. He died in 1864 of *angina pectoris* which, according to Mark Lemon, was the result of a disturbance to the nervous system brought on by 'the continual visitation of street-bands and organ-grinders'. Dickens said of Leech's works 'They were always the drawings of a gentleman'. Perhaps that was the trouble. He glorified the bourgeois in the hunting field, and no doubt delights members of the Jorrocks Society; but his satires lack bite.

Richard Doyle (1824–83) was a more irreverent and attractive caricaturist. He designed the ever-to-be-lamented original cover of *Punch*, with the horseman holding what may be a lictor's *fasces*, but which *Private Eye* has gleefully dubbed 'Punch's prick'. He invented the comic strip in the adventures of his three characters, Brown, Jones and Robinson. Like Bunbury, he was amazingly precocious: his first published work was *The Eglinton Tournament; or, the Days of Chivalry revived*, produced in his fifteenth year. Recently, with a revival of interest in Victorian surrealism, he has become well known for his 'fairyland' scenes: elves, ogres and fantastic combats. To *Punch* he contributed 'Manners and Customs of ye Englyshe, drawn from ye Quick by Richard Doyle'. It is the England of Thackeray, the young Dickens, Jenny Lind and cricketers in stove-pipe hats. In 1850 Doyle left *Punch* as he was a Roman Catholic and resented the magazine's attacks on Rome. His strong ethical sense also led him to refuse to illustrate the works of Swift, of which he disapproved; but he did illustrate the novels of Thackeray—who was also, incidentally, a clever amateur caricaturist.

Leech's successor as *Punch*'s leading caricaturist was John Tenniel (1820–1914). A modern *Punch* cartoonist, William Hewison, talking about Tenniel on the Home Service in 1964, said: 'His drawings of Alice, the Walrus, the Carpenter and the

Jabberwock seem to be so completely right that we tend to have a built-in prejudice against all other versions.' As the illustrator of *Alice*, Tenniel is sublime, but as a political caricaturist he is rarely more than dourly competent. He joined *Punch* in 1850 and during his fifty years' service drew over 2000 cartoons. But he hardly ever manages to transmute his subject into something new—as he was forced to do with the fantasy-creatures of Alice: the stolid, straight realism of his style gave verisimilitude to Carroll's imaginings, but adds nothing to our idea of, say, Bismarck, in Tenniel's most famous cartoon, *Dropping the Pilot* (1890).

Edward Linley Sambourne (1844–1910) succeeded Tenniel as the chief cartoonist of *Punch*. If Tenniel's illustrations to *Alice* are the canonical ones, so are Sambourne's designs for Kingsley's *The Water Babies*. They have something of the same gothic quality. 'How he, our comrade, with his pencil lent your fancy's speech a firmer spell,' as Sir Owen Seaman rather contortedly put it in *Punch* when Carroll died. Perhaps it was translation on to the woodblock that gave their cartoons and illustrations that angular, medieval quality. When one finds a Sambourne original, such as the decorated envelope and letter shown here, it has a racing impetuousness which the woodblock cartoons lack. Mr F. Gordon Roe, in his delightful book *Victorian Corners* calls this side of Sambourne's work an 'elegant prankishness'. He also refers to a rare photograph of Tenniel and Sambourne together, published in the *Daily Telegraph* on 14 March 1960, shortly before Princess Margaret's marriage to Sambourne's great-grandson, now Lord Snowdon (hence the title of his son, Viscount Linley).

Harry Furniss (1854–1925) also illustrated Lewis Carroll—the two *Sylvie and Bruno* books of 1889 and 1893. (Carroll confided to him that he hated all Tenniel's illustrations except for 'Humpty Dumpty'. As Furniss remarks, it was rather as if Gilbert had said he detested Sullivan's music.) Furniss is the most spirited of the Victorian cartoonists. His superabundant energy is shown in the letter of 1908 illustrated here, with its self-portrait and the sketches of Dickens (Furniss's hero—he evidently thought himself a Dickens of the crayon), Joseph Chamberlain, the many-chinned Sir William Harcourt and Gladstone in the enormous collars which,

Harry Furniss, letter of 1908 showing self-portrait and caricatures of (*left to right*), Dickens, Joseph Chamberlain, Sir William Harcourt and Gladstone *Author's collection*

THE MOUN...
HIGH WICKHA...
HASTINGS.

I have Charles Dickens — on the
train now! writing a book.
about my lecture on humour.

my family say. this is not a bit
like me! I have given myself
Too much of a "dome of thought" as
the Americans say. Yours and sincerely

J Harry Furniss

Phil May: 'Daddy's waistcoat' signed and dated 1895
The Fine Art Society, Ltd

Furniss once suggested, he grew in his shrubbery at Hawarden. He was a skilful political cartoonist. Over three hundred of his drawings are at the National Portrait Gallery. He also perpetrated a good 'artistic joke' as he called it, by hiring the Gainsborough Gallery and filling it with life-sized parodies of Royal Academicians' works (an Orchardson ship-deck with every floorboard minutely delineated; *The Ornithologist's Daughter*, by Stacy Marks; *I dreamed that I dwelt in Marble Halls* by Alma-Tadema, etc.). Of what Furniss considered his most successful political study, *The Academy* wrote:

In humour Mr Furniss generally excels; but his portrait of Lord Beaconsfield on his last appearance in the House of Commons is something more than amusing—it is pathetic, almost tragic, and will be historical.

Four other outstanding cartoonists served *Punch* with Furniss in the late nineteenth century: George Du Maurier (1834–96); Charles Keene (1823–91); Phil May (1864–1903) and Edward Tennyson Reed (1860–1933). Du Maurier, whose cartoon of 'the

Phil May (1864–1903) : 'If I was you I wouldn't 'ave anything to do with that Mrs Smithers, I think she ain't respectable' 1898 *The Fine Art Society, Ltd*

On pages 56 and 57
George Du Maurier (1834–96) : 'Cetewayo in London : Mrs Ponsonby de Tomkyns realises her life's ambition and receives Royalty in her own house' *John Lewis, Esq.*

Cetewayo

Mrs. *Ponsonby de Tomkyns et Cetewayo à un bal à la...*

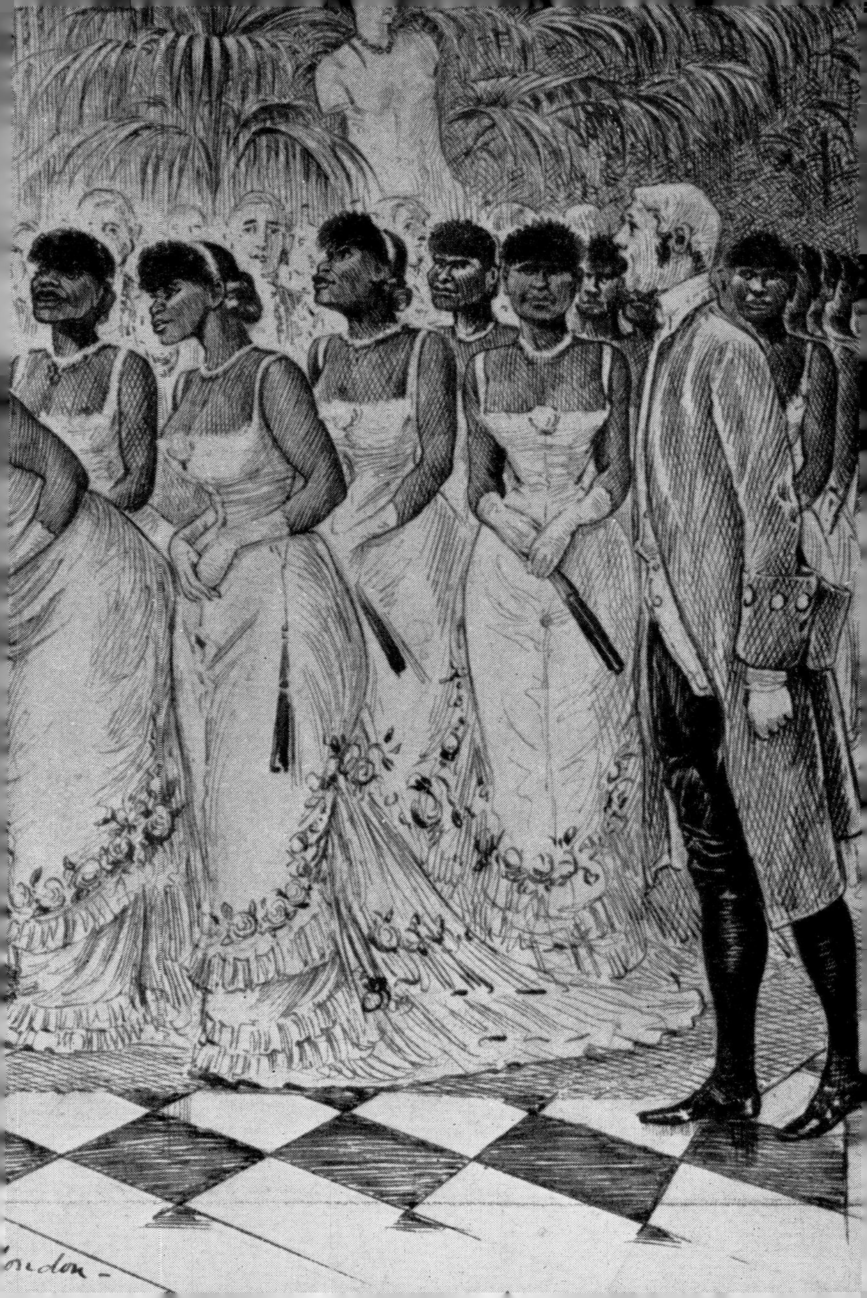

BRITANNIA À LA BEARDSLEY

By our 'Yellow' Decadent

Athleticism and aestheticism: cartoon by **Sir Francis Carruthers Gould** (1844–1925) in *Truth* 25 December 1890

curate's egg' added a new Familiar Phrase to the language, had two main targets: the *nouveau riche* middle classes, and the aesthetic movement led by Oscar Wilde. Keene and May both found their subjects in the cockney world of urchins, cabmen and slippered beldames—the one in a style of finished draughtsmanship, the other in a pictorial shorthand of marvellous verve and economy. Reed was primarily a political caricaturist, but like Du Maurier he enjoyed satirizing the aesthetes, and his parodies of Beardsley and the *Yellow Book* cover are delicious. He was a

'Political Ally Sloper' by **W. G. Baxter** *The Fine Art Society, Ltd*

literary caricaturist too ; his autobiographical fragments, edited by
Sir Shane Leslie, should not be missed by any historian of late
Victorian and Edwardian England.

It is a curious general rule of caricature that the best draughts-
men often have the weakest sense of humour—and *vice-versa*.
Sir Francis Carruthers Gould (1844–1925) is an example of a
hopelessly crude draughtsman with wit and panache. He was a
stockbroker and only an amateur cartoonist until 1879, when he
was asked by H. Voules to illustrate the Christmas number of
Henry Labouchère's inaptly named journal *Truth*. He continued to
illustrate the Christmas numbers until 1895. Gould's cartoon
images, from their very lack of subtlety, tended to stick : he was the
precursor of Low and Vicky rather than Steadman or Scarfe. The
only politician who eluded him was John Morley, whose bland,
donnish face had no outstanding feature, and who was not
obliging enough to wear an orchid, like the almost as inscrutable
Joseph Chamberlain, or a monocle like Sir Walter Barttelot Barttelot, Bart. (a real politician and not a figment of imagination).

There were other rivals to *Punch* apart from *Truth* (which ranked as the *Private Eye* of its day.) *Punch* was a middle-class magazine. For the working class there was the halfpenny paper, *Ally Sloper's Half-Holiday*. Ally Sloper, with his knobbly knees and syphilitic nose, became a cult figure in 'upper Bohemia' too : William Morris and Burne-Jones, among others, enjoyed his antics, drawn by Marie Duval and W. G. Baxter. Then there was *Fun*, or the 'penny *Punch*' as it was known. *Fun* was owned by Edward Wylam until 1870, when he went into the dog-biscuit industry instead. It was then taken over by the brothers Dalziel, wood-engravers. Its best cartoonist was James F. Sullivan, who sometimes signed himself 'Jassef' (for Jas. F.) A cartoonist of advanced radical ideas, he was one of the first to take a jaundiced view of Victorian imperialism : one of his comic strips shows Africa being 'opened up', first by force of arms, then by factory-building in the name of Christianity and charity.

One magazine specialized in personal caricature of the old Dighton type : *Vanity Fair*. Most of the caricatures by 'Ape' (Carlo Pellegrini) and 'Spy' (Sir Leslie Ward), were so highly finished that they are only slightly distorted academic pictures. 'Ape', who was the better artist, was a familiar figure in 'Bohemian' society. He turns up in Frank Harris's *My Life and Loves*. Harris, who was introduced to him by Alfred Tennyson, the poet's son, wrote :

Carlo confessed to being a homosexualist, flaunted his vice, indeed, and was the first to prove to me by example that a perverted taste in sex might go with a sweet and generous nature. For Carlo Pellegrini was one of nature's saints. One trait I must give: once every fortnight he went to the office of *Vanity Fair* in the Strand and drew twenty pounds for his cartoon. He had only a couple of hundred yards to go before reaching Charing Cross and usually owed his landlady five pounds; yet he had seldom more than five pounds left out of the twenty by the time he got to the end of the street. I have seen him give five pounds to an old prostitute and add a kindly word to his gift. . . . The best thing I can say of the English aristocracy is that this member and that remained his friend throughout his career. . . . Lord Rosebery was one of his kindliest patrons, my friend Tennyson was another. . . . In person he was a grotesque caricature of humanity, hardly more than five feet two in height, squat and stout, with a face like a mask of Socrates, and always curiously ill-dressed ; yet always and everywhere a gentleman—and to those who knew him, a good deal more.

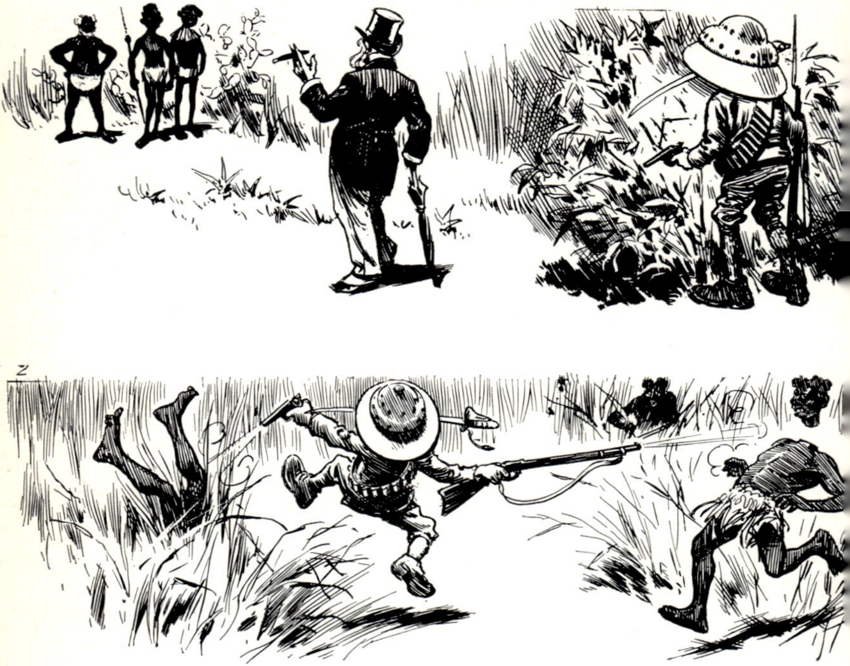

Strip Cartoon by **James Sullivan** for *Fun. From originals in the author's collection*

Pellegrini (1839–89), who was born at Capua, had fought with Garibaldi at Capua and Volturno. He came to London in 1864 and began working for *Vanity Fair* in 1869. Harry Furniss, in *My Bohemian Days* (1919) has described how 'Ape' asked Disraeli's secretary Monty Corry (Lord Rowton) whether he would persuade the old statesman to give him a sitting. 'Can't be done, Carlo,' was the reply. 'But I'll trot him out of doors for you tomorrow, and walk him up and down till you have made your sketch, and he will be none the wiser.' Furniss called his own sketch of this incident, reproduced here, '*Ape*' *catching the last of Beaconsfield*.

When 'Ape' was offered a subject he did not relish, he would say, according to 'Spy', 'I don't like 'im. Send Ward—'e can run after 'im better.' 'Spy' (Sir Leslie Ward, 1851–1922) thought continually of those who were truly great. His memoirs are a marathon of name-dropping and tedious recollections of his famous sitters. He lacked 'Ape's' flair. It was left to Max Beerbohm (1872–1956) to pare down and refine the *Vanity Fair* style into a new simplified manner which would break completely with the old tradition by which caricature was merely an adaptation (to many, an inferior one) of the academic portrait.

Max was the greatest wit ever to apply his cunning to caricature. His draughtsmanship was not contemptible, but he had none of the virtuosity of Furniss or even the academic facility of Tenniel. What he did have was an understanding that, if caricature was to have any point, it must be some kind of alternative to straight portraiture, must break with the portrait-miniature style of 'Ape' and 'Spy'. He applied to caricature the techniques of the literary epigrammatist. He had been with Wilde when the latter sent back a sandwich on the grounds that he had asked for a watercress sandwich, 'not a loaf with a field in the middle of it'. This was the kind of hyperbole he introduced in caricature. If Mr Swinburne had a large head and a rather puny body, Max would show him as a rufous-headed tadpole. If Mr Balfour was tall and attenuated, Max would stretch him out like pyjama elastic. The morbid medieval antics of the Pre-Raphaelites were for the first time mocked in their arty-crafty stronghold, where pale ladies of the Birmingham Guild of Handicraft reverently guarded their hand-woven ideas: mocked by a puckish aesthete who knew just how to tip Rossetti and his friends from their Morris workshop pedestals. Rossetti's

' "Ape" catching the last of Beaconsfield': cartoon by **Harry Furniss** of Carlo Pellegrini sketching Disraeli who is being taken for a walk by Montagu Corry (Lord Rowton)

pet wombats; 'Topsy' and 'Ned' settled on the settle at Red Lion Square; Coventry Patmore expostulating over a teapot—these, together with all the jolly slang and practical jokery of Pre-Raphaelite life, he exposed to sweet eternal ridicule. Even where his drawing (which owed something to Edward Lear's limerick illustrations and even more to Aubrey Beardsley) is uncertain, the captions are usually exquisitely apt. Mr Justice Darling, who was renowned for his misplaced sense of humour at murder trials, is shown handing the black cap to a marshal: 'Oh, and get some bells sewn on this cap, will you?' In *Evenings in Printing House Square*, the staff of *The Times* race to restrain Lord Northcliffe, who shouts: 'Help! Again I feel the demons of sensationalism rising in me. Hold me fast! Curb me, if you love me!'

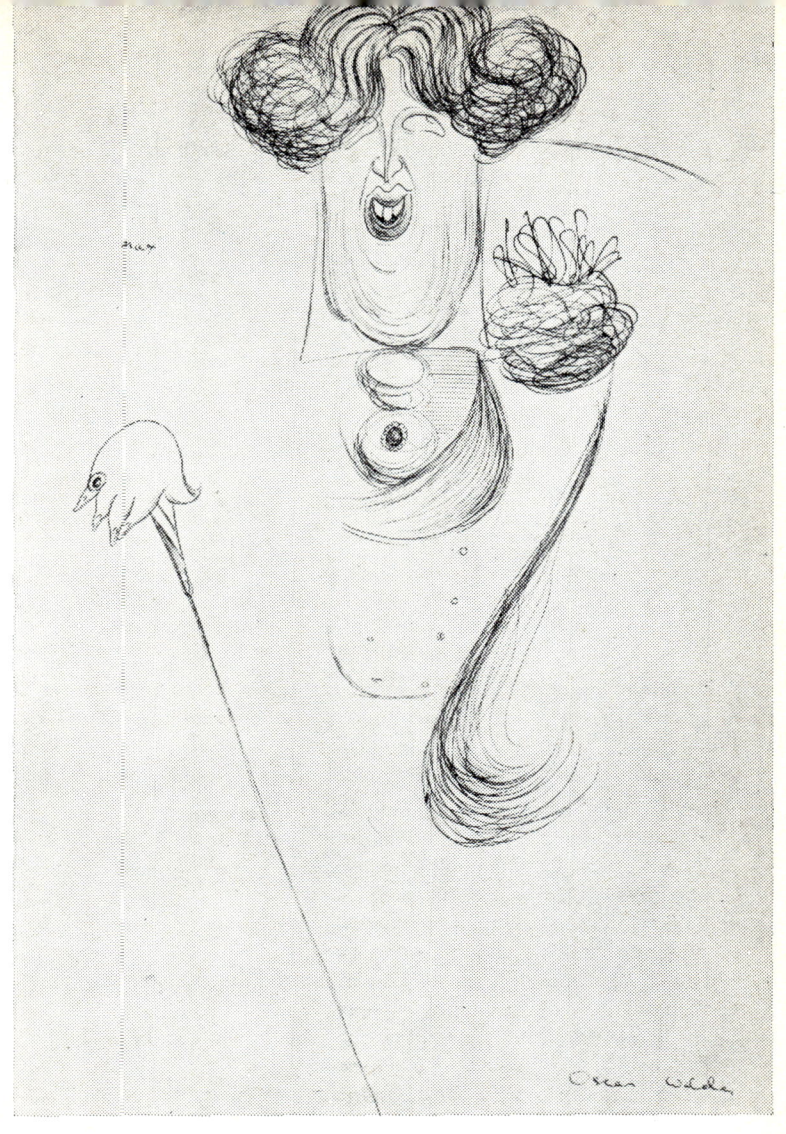

Max Beerbohm: Oscar Wilde *Ashmolean Museum, Oxford*

Max Beerbohm (1872–1956) : Reginald Turner

Max achieved a pastel-coloured revolution. With the exception of a few dogged survivors such as Bernard Partridge, British cartoonists of the twentieth century jettisoned the old Tenniel–Sambourne–Furniss paraphernalia of pen-and-ink cross-hatching and shading, and the 'Ape'–'Spy' apparatus of waxy moulding, and adopted Max's technique of eloquent outline, sometimes filled with flats of colour. We are only now beginning to see the first signs of revolt against this regimen, in the caricatures of David Levine in America, with their confessed debt to Tenniel. Max himself will remain a caricaturist for connoisseurs. To the typical Max caricature one can apply what the *Manchester Guardian* said of his Oxford novel *Zuleika Dobson* when it appeared in 1908 :

The figure may look like bisque, but the pedestal is rock ; and good old laws, observed austerely, run up through the ribands and the garlands and the tinted coquetries to sustain the poised caprice.

Germany: Daniel Chodowiecki

The first half of the eighteenth century was a barren period for caricature in Germany. Published caricature was virtually limited to reprints of the pictorial satire of other countries, such as Oesterreich's engravings after Ghezzi (1750) and a few prints mocking Frederick William I and his bear. The impulse for a caricature revival came from England. The prints of Hogarth had a wide circulation on the Continent, and in 1773 Daniel Chodowiecki (1726–1806) published a series of engravings of *The Rake's Progress*, of which the debt to Hogarth's series of 1735, although denied by Chodowiecki in a letter of 1779, is obvious.

Types of Berlin ecclesiastics by **Chodowiecki**

Wallfahrt nach Frantzöß. Buchholz   *gezeichnet von D. Chodowiecki in Berlin 1775*

Cavalcade by **Chodowiecki,** 1775

But to call Chodowiecki, as one French historian has done, *le Hogarth Berlinois*, is hardly fair to Hogarth. Chodowiecki's demure vignettes, engraved with fussy little strokes of the burin, never approach the exuberance of Hogarth's style. And in general Chodowiecki satirized high society. Whatever the Berlin equivalent of *Gin Lane* may have been, it was not thought fit for his delicate delineation. His interest was in the *passions douces*, in new modes, the fopperies of ecclesiastics, the *ennui* of *mariages de convenance*, travesties of the Aeneid which might bring a frigid smile to the lips of a classical scholar. He was happy satirizing the medieval gothic in fashion at Berlin; the princes, princicules and principuscules of the German states; the Jesuits; Austrian diplomacy—but there is in his work little of the personal satire of Hogarth. He was much more in his element illustrating *Don Quixote* and Sterne's *Sentimental Journey* (Sterne was as popular in Germany as Hogarth). Between 1780 and 1802 he engraved more than 2000 caricatures. At his best, he has the charm of the super-civilized, but he has been overrated, especially by German writers. He had a small school of followers, chief of whom was David Hess.

Portrait of Daniel Chodowiecki (1726–1806), painted by **A. Graff,** engraved by F. Arnold

Influence of physiognomy and the silhouette

Caricaturists are not easily influenced by general developments in thought, writing or art: it is, after all, their métier to be cynical about such things, to expose and satirize them. But two eighteenth-century innovations did have a lasting effect on the art of caricature. One was the expounding of the science of physiognomy by Lavater. In 1775 he published the results of his researches into the human face. The new science, he claimed, enabled one 'to know the inner man by the outer, to apprehend the invisible by the visible surface'. And that is surely the essence of caricature. Lavater was himself an accomplished draughtsman, but because he wanted the best illustrations obtainable, he commissioned them from Chodowiecki. Lavater had stringent ideas of caricature. The caricaturist should not depict the *lusus naturae*, or 'make a caricature of that which in nature seems already a caricature'. Neither should he merely distort the disagreeable features, omitting the

Louis Philippe and the pear, by **Charles Philipon**

Page from **Lavater's** *Physiognomy*

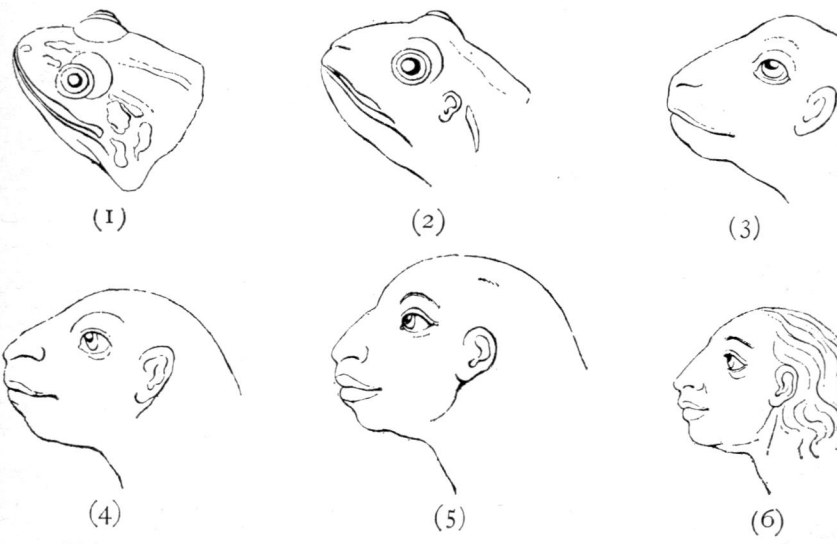

(1) (2) (3)

(4) (5) (6)

finer traits. To Leonardo's *anatomie du laid*, Lavater opposed an *anatomie du beau*. He also invented a technique of showing the degrees by which animal creation gradually approached human creation—frog into prince, monkey into Sir Isaac Newton. It was a weird, vague anticipation of Darwin's law of evolution. This technique of successive transitions became one of the favourite tricks of German caricature; though the best known example is the transition from prince to pear, in Charles Philipon's caricature of Louis Philippe and the pear.

71

An eighteenth-century parody of silhouette

The satirists and caricaturists had their fun at Lavater's expense. The last volume of his great work had hardly appeared, in 1778, when Lichtenberg and Musaeus published, respectively, their *Sur la physiognomie, contre les physiognomistes* and *Voyages physiognomiques,* pushing Lavater's theories to the last limits of the absurd. The most telling satire on Lavater was called 'Fragments of Queues', first published in Baldinger's *New Magazine of Medecine*. This was illustrated with the *queues* of piglets and British bulldogs—even that of Henry VIII's dog, whose tail conveyed, according to the spoof physiognomist, an attitude of *Aut Caesar aut nihil*. The reader was asked to suggest which was the most powerful of all the *queues*—where that of the jurist, the doctor or theologian was to be identified, which was the most amorous, Goethe's or that which Homer might choose if he returned to the world.

Silhouette by **G. Hoale,** from *Lustigen Blätter*, 1906

The science of physiognomy led naturally to the art of silhouette. Lavater said in his work on physiognomy that no art approached the exactness of a well executed silhouette. Miniature painters went out of business as the mania for silhouettes spread. Conventional portraitists railed against the *'personnages à l'ombre noire'* and the *'canaille pantographique'*. Once again, the caricaturists were ready with retaliation: malicious drawings suggesting the discrepancy between actual profiles and flattering silhouettes. Chodowiecki penned and illustrated a caustic couplet in his mangled Germanic French:

> *L'art de silhoueter est admirable!*
> *Tout chat est noir pendant la nuit.*

Yet silhouette was to become one of the favourite techniques of the caricaturist. It is seen at its best in the nineteenth century, in

'Laetitia in the Conservatory' by **Harry Furniss** (illustration for Frank Burnand's *Happy Thoughts*, 1890 edition)

F. Barnard's illustrations to Mark Twain's *My Watch* in *The World of Wit and Humour*, edited by George Manville Fenn; in the political silhouettes of Henry Labouchère's magazine, *Truth*; in Harry Furniss's greenery-yallery illustrations to F. C. Burnand's *Happy Thoughts* (1890 edition), and, in the twentieth century, G. Hoale's military silhouettes for the 1906 *Lustigen Blätter* and the margin decorations of the 1920s *La Vie Parisienne*. Silhouette was also used with imagination in various comic alphabets, such as the anonymous set of 'Shadows', printed by F. Elliot of Holywell Street, the Strand, used on the cover of the present book.

Title-page of 'Silhouettes' by **Theodor von Kramer**

Germany: the nineteenth century

German caricature in the nineteenth century had a course similar to that of the eighteenth : a period of comparative sterility, followed about the middle of the century by a sudden flowering inspired by foreign example. It is true that some outstanding examples do survive from the earlier years of the century: for instance, the humorous sketches of Napoleon and his generals by Johann Gottfried Schadow (1764–1850), rector of the Academy of Fine Arts in Berlin. Another exception was the polymath Ernest Theodor Wilhelm Hoffmann (1776–1822), a magistrate at Glogau (1796), at Berlin (1798–1800) and at Varsovie (1800–6); director in 1808 of the theatre of Bamberg where he was at the same time leader of the orchestra; critic for a Leipzig newspaper; and then, from 1813–14, director of a new opera theatre playing alternatively at Leipzig and Dresden. The very opposite of Chodowiecki's caricatures, his were predominantly personal satires, sketches of real people, not types. As a comic draughtsman, he was as facile and prolific as in all his other talents. A friend of his took a portfolio of his caricatures to a masked ball; everyone present was handed a caricature of someone else present. At first there was a general chuckle of contentment in the ballroom; then, as everyone found a caricature of himself in the hand of a neighbour, laughter gave place to fury, and the culprit was sought. He, of course, was present, well masked. In 1813 Hoffmann drew and had engraved a series of caricatures of Napoleon and the *maudits Français*. He wrote and illustrated, with equal raillery, several books : *The famous minister Klein-Zach* (1819), *Personal Impressions of the cat Kater-Murr* (1821), *The maître de chappelle Jean Kreisler* (1822) and volumes pastiching the caprices of Callot. German caricatures tend to be heavily stylized, in the manner of early woodcuts: uncompromising outlines, stiff draperies like linen-fold panelling, staid marionette gestures. Hoffmann is outside this tradition. His drawings have a freedom and vivacity which put him in the class of Rowlandson, or the David of the Marie Antoinette sketch (see p. 94).

But the great period of German caricature did not begin until around the Revolution of 1848, when a number of new satirical journals was founded: at Munich, *Fliegende Blätter* (1845),

Theodor Wilhelm Hoffman (1776–1822) : Kreisler, mad. (from the third volume of *Kater-Murr*)

Punsch (named after its English cousin in 1847) and *Leucht-kugeln* (1848), which was suppressed by the authorities in 1851 ; at Stuttgart, *Eulenspiegel* (1851) ; at Mainz, *Narhalla* (1860) ; the *Leipziger Charivari* (1858) and the *Berliner Charivari* (1847), soon followed, also at Berlin, by *Kladderadatsch* (1848). Of these, *Kladderadatsch* in the north, and *Leuchtkugeln* in the south soon became the most important.

Kladderadatsch had the unique distinction of having its title suggested by a dog. The magazine's founder, D. Kalisch, was talking over possibilities for a title with one of his staff at dinner, when a dog knocked a pile of plates off the table. 'Kladderadatsch !' cried one of the men (how typical, linguistically, that the French word for crash ! should be *patatras !* and the German, *Kladderadatsch !*) The word was adopted and turned out to be an apt title. Kalisch was so grateful to the dog that he had a dog's head incorporated into the right cheek of the jolly boy's face on the journal's cover. A case of *Cherchez le chien*.

The cover of the magazine *Kladderadatsch*, founded in 1848, with detail showing the dog incorporated into the boy's face

The magazine began with a ramping editorial (1 May 1848): 'The elections have taken place; the princes are routed; thrones reversed; women honoured; Jews emancipated; priests discredited—Kladderadatsch!' While *Kladderadatsch* trumpeted the triumph of Berlin democracy, the magazines of the south, *Leuchtkugeln* in Munich and *Eulenspiegel* in Stuttgart, showed the general spirit of German political caricature more clearly; for Frankfort remained the centre of publications directed against the famous Parliament whose feebleness and vacillation could lose the national cause.

Napoleon III cutting the German cake; *Punsch*, 1866

Kladderadatsch and *Punsch* for politics, *Fliegende Blätter* for the *comédie humaine*: these three were the dominant caricature magazines in Germany in the second half of the nineteenth century. From 1852 to 1871 they were obsessed with Napoleon III, who had come to the throne in France with the re-establishment of the Bonaparte dynasty in 1851. He was shown balanced on the world holding a rod labelled 'Despotismus'; as a pâtissier cutting the German cake; dancing the cancan with Italy, Hungary and Poland; personifying proverbs, or compared with the great Napoleon: the eagle's egg and the cuckoo's egg.

Napoleon defeated and dethroned, the political magazines lost

The eagle's egg and the cuckoo's egg *The Industrial Humourist* 1869

some of their bite. *Punsch* disappeared, and no new journal took its place. *Kladderadatsch* could invent no Aunt Sally with half the hate-appeal of Napoleon III. As J. Grand-Carteret wrote : 'Il semble que tout l'esprit de ses dessinateurs ait disparu avec celui qu'il habilla de tant d'épithetes différentes, mais qu'il sut à la fois ridiculiser et populariser si bien de l'autre côté du Rhin, créant un type qui restera éternellement vrai.' (It seemed that all the spirit of its artists had disappeared with him whom it had dressed in so many different disguises but whom it knew at once how to mock and popularize so well from the other side of the Rhine, creating a type which will remain eternally true.')

Eduard Ille: vignette for E. Bormann's poems

M. von Schwind: vignette for *Philosophic Aphorisms*

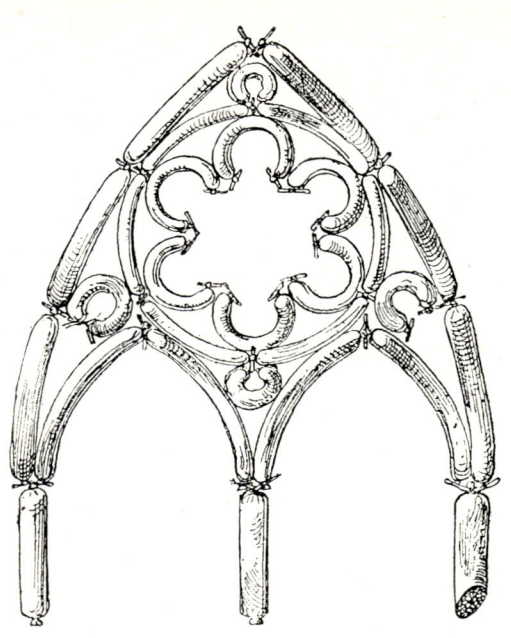

Architecture saucissonnière (Schalk)

With these artists, we begin to notice a change in the style of caricature—a new simplicity. The abandoning of complex shading and cross-hatching, and the use of a pure outline is one of the main characteristics of neo-classicism; and if one looks at Johann Overbeck's illustrations to Ferdinand Lachmann's translation of Sophocles' tragedies (Leipzig, 1873), one gets some idea of how dominant neo-classicism was in Germany at that time. But the

'Diana hunting', a caricature by **Oberländer**

caricatures of Oberländer and Meggendorfer take us a stage further. There is a mischievous abandon in Oberländer's *Diana hunting*, which, taken with its vaudeville neo-classicism, anticipates Picasso's lithographs. Caricaturists have often proved that rigid academic precepts are for the guidance of the intelligent and imaginative, and for the implicit obedience of fools.

'The frog and the lieutenant', caricature by **Oberländer**

The mode of the day, or an excusable error: 'Ah, charming, this old furniture!'
Caricature by **L. Bechstein**

With the caricatures of Wilhelm Busch (born 1832 at Wiedensahl, Hanover) we arrive at the ultimate simplicity, the final distillation. To those who know Busch only from the rather nudgingly whimsical, pawky little drawings which form the vast bulk of his work, this might seem an extravagant claim. France's André Gill, or our own George Cruikshank (who indeed has much in common with Busch, down to the wildly fantasticated signature each affected) produced work more skilful and more risible. Two clairvoyant scribbles are all that mark out Busch as an inspired innovator. They establish him as the first true modern of the art.

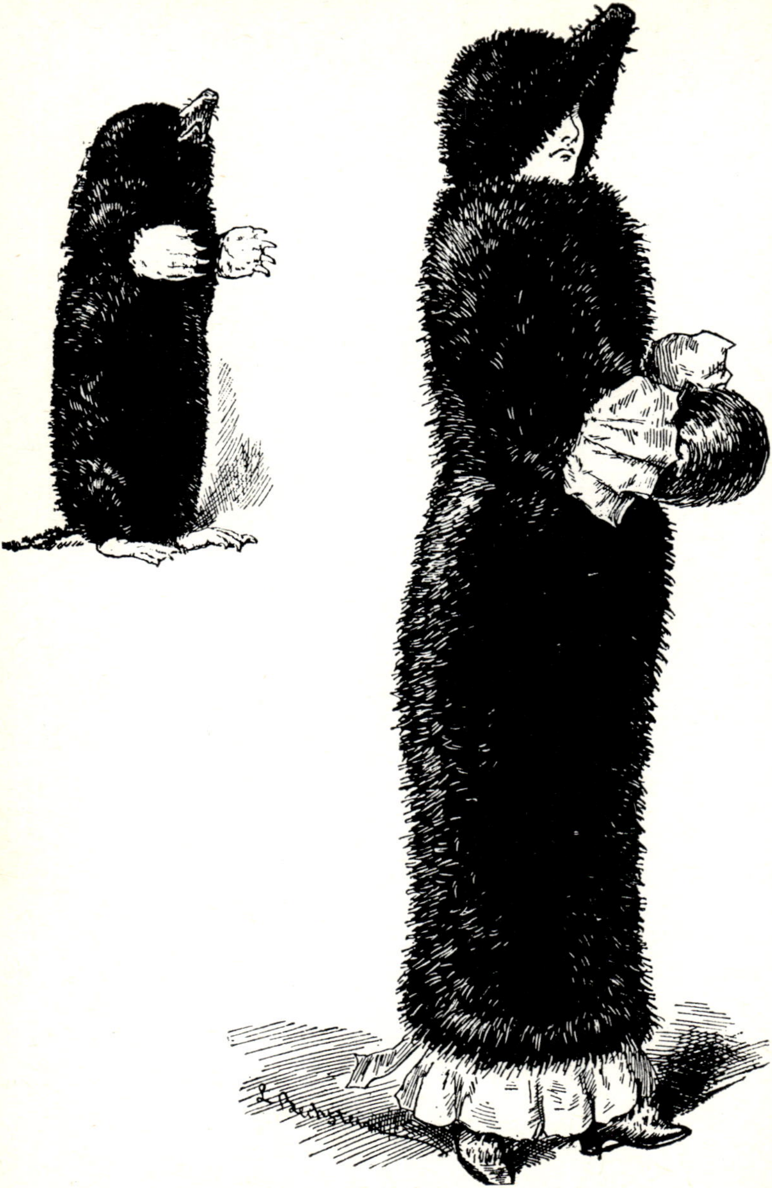

Caricatures of fashion by **L. Bechstein**

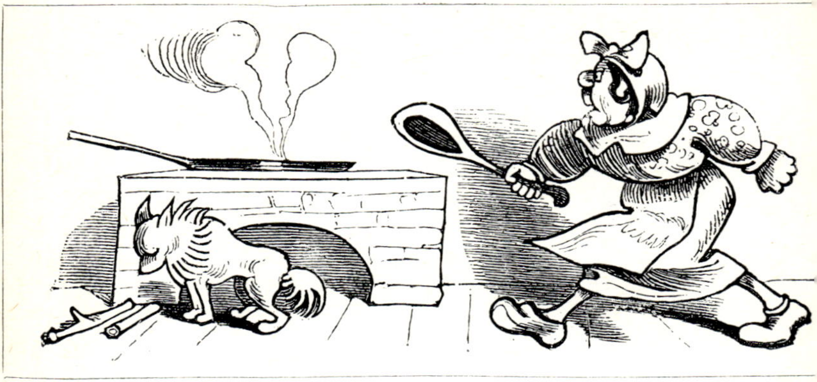

Wilhelm Busch: vignette from 'Max und Moritz'

Wilhelm Busch: drawing Frederick the Great

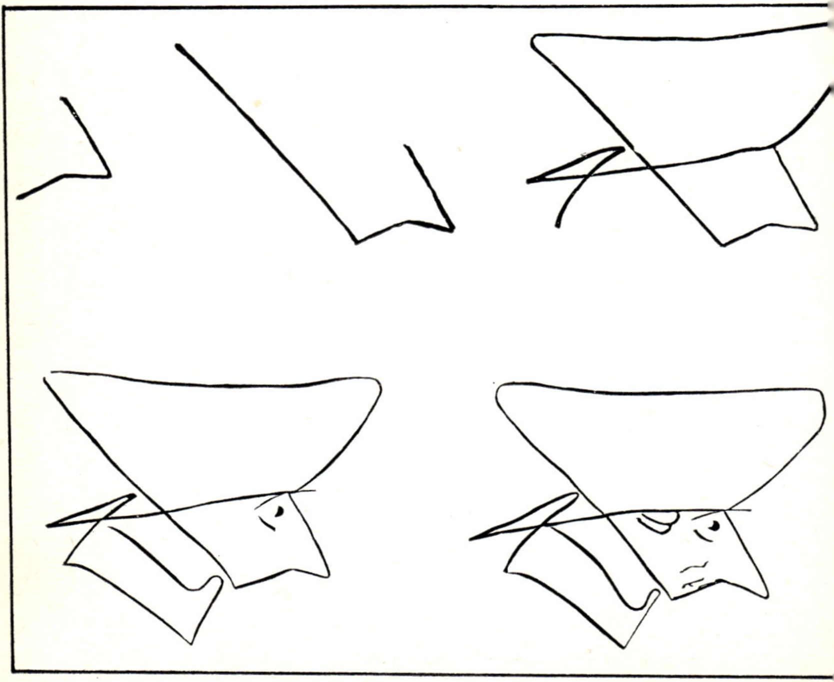

Portraits of (*left to right*) Meggendorfer, Busch and Oberländer

These are his 'progressive' portraits of Frederick the Great and of Napoleon. Beginning with an apparently wayward line, he doodles two portraits of perfect conviction: the foxy lineaments of Frederick sandwiched between a great hat and collar; the frustrated power of Napoleon at Waterloo, paraded in the misplaced pretentiousness of his half-moon hat. These featherlight sketches were literally 'strokes of genius'. They were an advance showing of what Paul Klee meant when he said: 'I let a line go for a walk'.

France: the Revolution to 1900

Naturally enough, the French Revolution was more caricatured in England than in France. The French either applauded the course of events, or kept quiet, or the guillotine claimed them. Sometimes moderates would attack extremists, or Girondins savage Jacobins, in clandestine caricatures: 'Robespierre guillotining the executioner' was one of the more sardonic commentaries. The revolutionaries also commissioned propaganda caricatures against priests, émigrés and the royal family, especially after the flight to Varennes in June 1791. But it was left to English artists to express abhorrence of the course the Revolution took. Gillray, who, like Fox and many other Englishmen, had been delighted by the fall of the Bastille and the sympathetic 'principles of 1789', was soon disillusioned, and produced a caricature of the execution of Louis XVI in 1793 entitled *The Zenith of French Glory*: the principal figure in the foreground is a Phrygian-bonneted *enragé*, sansculottes, sitting in the glass bowl of a *lanterne* on which a priest and a monk are strung up. The king's head is in the guillotine, and the blade, emblazoned with the royal crest, is about to fall as the executioner mans the winch. At the top of the page, Gillray has labelled this composition 'A view in perspective'—which can be taken both literally and as a sad admission that the principles of 1789 did not seem so sympathetically liberal with the perspective of time.

But it was the queen's fate that provoked the most poignant French caricature of the Revolution: David's sketch of Marie-Antoinette on the way to the guillotine. Her shorn head is in a mob-cap and her mouth is pursed in an expression of furious resignation. Opinions differ as to the feelings which prompted David's caricature. J. M. Thompson, in his *The French Revolution*, cites the 'cruel sketch' as evidence of David's implacable animus: not content with voting for her death, he would hound her to it with his crayon. On the other hand, Hugh Honour, in his book *Neo-Classicism* has written:

Yet David seems never to have become a fanatically doctrinaire Jacobin. His drawing of Marie Antoinette on her way to the guillotine reveals his tenderness for the woman, however much he

Thomas Gillray: 'The Zenith of French Glory' 1793

A View in Perspective.

Zenith of French Glory; _ The Pinnacle of Liberty.

...n Justice Loyalty & all the Bugbears of Unenlighten'd Minds, Farewell!

Jacques-Louis David: sketch of Marie-Antoinette on her way to the guillotine 1793 *Paris, Louvre*

may have hated and despised the Queen for whose execution he had voted. It reminds one of Baudelaire's phrase—that David had *'quelquechose de tendre et poignant à la fois'*.

There are few occasions when anyone writing on art would wish to disagree with Mr Honour, but one does not need to be an impassioned partisan of Marie-Antionette, like Burke, or a sentimental biographer making literary capital out of her death, like Hilaire Belloc, to suspect that David harboured no very tender feelings for her as either woman or queen.

Honoré Daumier: Europe balancing on a live bomb

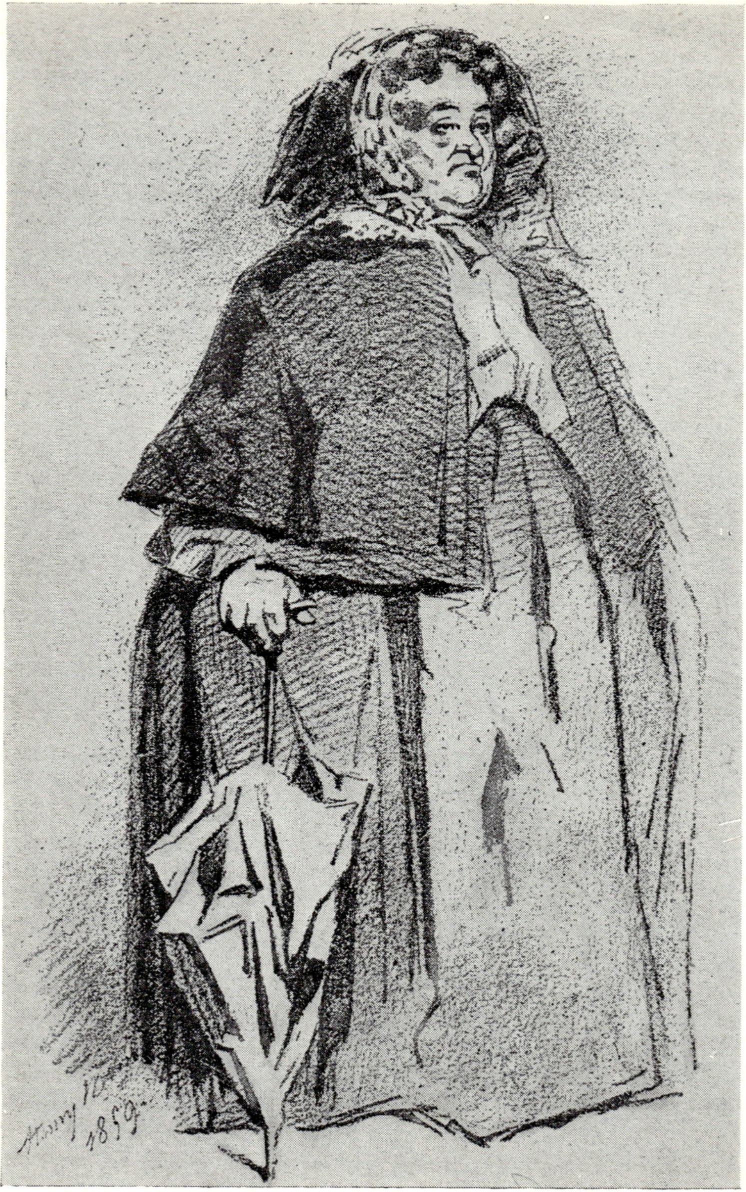

After the Revolution there was a period of reaction, of indulgence in outlandish fashion and a frenetic gaiety similar to that which overtook France and England after the First World War in the Roaring Twenties. Isabey, a pupil of David, and caricaturists such as Carle Vernet, Bosio and Boilly, satirized the monstrous costumes of the *Incroyables*, the *Merveilleuses* and the *Invisibles* (so named because of their huge poke bonnets into which, the caricaturists suggested, men had to thrust their heads, as into a tunnel, for any chance of conversation.)

In 1830, French caricature formed a new alliance with the press. A young man named Charles Philipon—he who was to turn Louis Philippe into a pear—founded the magazine *La Caricature*, whose contributors included Daumier, Grandville (real name Gérard), Decamps, Monnier, Traviès (Charles Joseph Traviès de Villers) and Gavarni (Sulpice Paul Chevalier). Daumier gained early notoriety; he was imprisoned in 1832 for a caricature of Louis Philippe as 'Gargantua'. Philipon was not deterred. In one year alone, *La Caricature* withstood 54 actions. It was succeeded by *Charivari*, the magazine on which *Punch* was based. Following another prosecution of Daumier for showing Lafayette asleep with a gigantic pear weighing on his chest, Philipon impudently had an account of all his legal troubles set by the printer in the shape of a pear.

To call Daumier a caricaturist is rather like calling Luca della Robbia a potter. He was the artist as caricaturist, not the other way round. His genius for caricature is perhaps seen at its best in his bronzes, such as *Ratapoil*, which showed that three-dimensional caricature could be taken further than leering gargoyles. He was merciless in his sculptured and lithographed satire on doctors and lawyers, but was also capable of compassion within the caricature manner, as his vignette of the effects of cholera proves.

The other illustrators of *La Caricature* and of *Charivari* were almost bound to be influenced by Daumier. Grandville was a sub-Daumier: though that was not a bad thing to be. Monnier's style was similar, but he contributed the complacent bourgeois figures of M. Joseph Prudhomme and Madame Prudhomme—a French Mrs Proudie. What from Daumier was power, could seem ponderous when it came from the crayon of Grandville or Monnier. Pigal

'Madame Prudhomme' by **Monnier**

Academician and Dancer by **Pigal**

(1794–1872) and Traviès (1804–59) contributed lighter, more skittish talents. Both made use of that ancient convention of caricature, the dwarf. Pigal has dwarf Academicians and dancers; one of Traviès's hunchback homunculi compares himself with a statue of Napoleon.

Constantin Guys, with his free style so suitable for lightning sketches on the battlefield (he contributed drawings of the Crimea to the *Illustrated London News*) and Gavarni, with his astutely observed scenes of high and low life in Paris, were also of the Daumier school. The heavy chiaroscuro—the school's main characteristic—was still present in the serious social satire and even the comic *jeux d'esprit* of Cham (his real name was Amédée de Noé, son of the Comte de Noé: hence 'Cham', or Shem, son of Noah.) And it continued to give grandeur to the style of Gustave Doré, one of whose books, the *Historical Cartoons* of 1868 (subtitled 'Rough pencillings of the World's History from the First to the Nineteenth Century') had a text by Thomas Wright, the author of an early history of caricature.

C-J. Traviès: 'Tonnerre de D . . . comme je lui ressemble l'

Gavarni: 'Phèdre at the Théâtre-Français: début of M. Paul des Trois-Etoiles, in the role of Hippolyte.'

Gavarni: 'This is a rotten show . . . it's disgusting . . . You haven't anything here, have you?' 'Good God, no I' 'Nor me'

'Cham': Fusion of two exhibitions, sculpture and flowers. (The old woman says: 'How inferior to flowers! Sculpture doesn't smell at all!')

André Gill: self portrait (which, however, he signed with the name of a friend, Augustine)

Another of Philipon's discoveries was André Gill (1840–85), whose name at birth was Louis-Alexandre Gosset, to which he later added 'de Guines' in the belief that he was the illegitimate son of the Comte de Guines. Gill was the inventor of the caricature style of large heads on midget bodies, which Max Beerbohm, among others, later adopted. His taste was for caricature pure and simple: physiognomy, not politics. His wraith-like Sarah Bernhardt, with gauzy wings and a body dwindling to a fluttering pennant of chiffon; his Wagner hammering at an ear with a crotchet; his bulging Balzac, screeching Madame Theresa and plethoric Bismarck are images so powerful that, once seen, they can easily overlay the true portraits one may have seen, as Lytton Strachey's literary caricatures of Newman, Manning, Florence Nightingale and General Gordon are alleged to do.

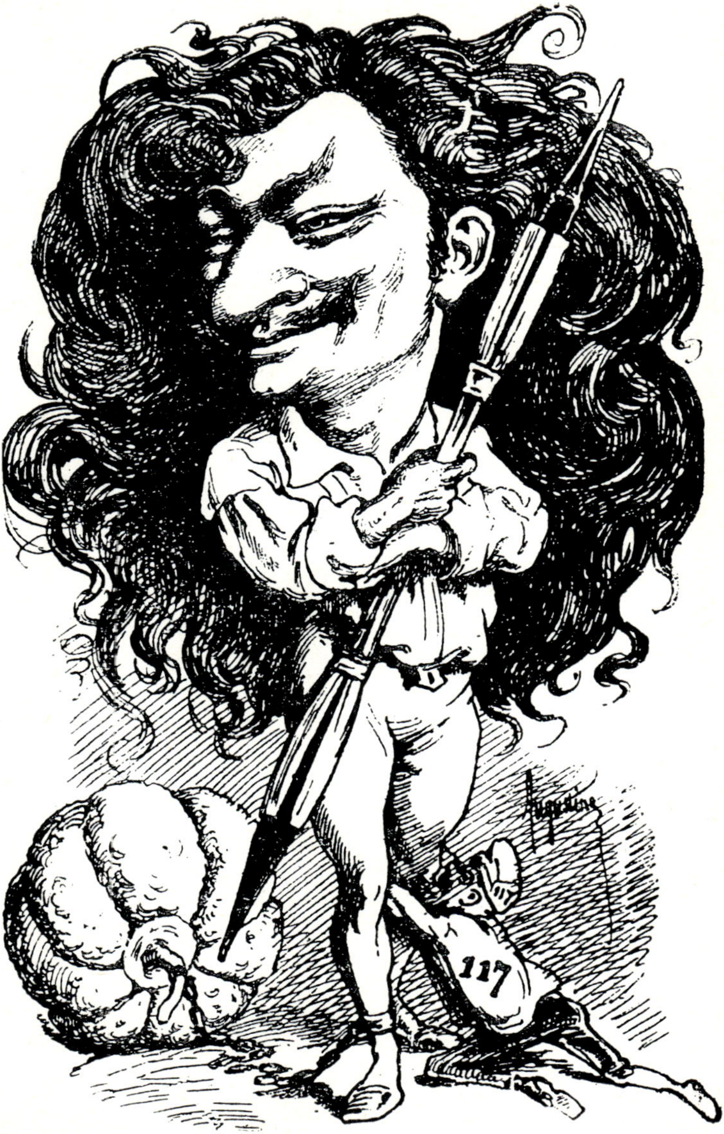
117

Léonce Petit: the promenade of the brothers *Journal Amusant*

But like Philipon's other satellites, Gill is still in the Daumier-esque, chiaroscuro tradition. What French artists now needed was a caricaturist who, like Wilhelm Busch in Germany, could lead them out of the shadows into a new style of crisp outline, of positive statements, unconfused by mazes of intersecting lines. Léonce Petit (1839–84) achieved this simplicity in his charming drawings of village scenes. But the man who established it was Caran d'Ache (Russian for 'pencil': his real name was Emmanuel Poirée). With J-L. Forain, who followed his lead with a looser linear style, he contributed in 1898–9 to a periodical called *Psst!*, mainly concerned with the Dreyfus scandal. Caran d'Ache's drawings are beautifully precise. There is no groping, no choosing from a tangle of tentative lines; this exactness, and the brio with which it is committed to paper, makes his preposterous situation-comedies convincing: for example the British general who is conferring with his chief of staff when the latter is blown to smithereens by the

André Gill: 'L'Avenir lui sourit'

H-G. Ibels: singer

arrival of a shell: 'Boy, sweep up the chief-of-staff and send me his assistant.' Caran d'Ache was the first caricaturist to introduce pithy captions, to replace the tiresome one-act-plays with which artists such as Du Maurier thought it necessary to gloss their drawings. The new linear simplicity derived partly from the Japanese print, partly from Aubrey Beardsley, and partly from the earlier book illustrations of Walter Crane and Randolph Caldecott, which had a great vogue in both Germany and France (even turning up in Huysmans's *A Rebours*.) It remained the favourite style of *fin de siècle* artists such as Willette and Ibels, although chiaroscuro was again adopted by the Flemish artist Félicien Rops for his satanic parodies. It was the style of Toulouse-Lautrec, whose letters are full of delightful caricatures, often of himself. And it was the style of the 1890s poster, in which simplicity was the

Caran d'Ache: two scenes from a duelling piece

Félicien Rops: 'A scene of animal magnetism'

Fin de siècle 'caricature for caricature's sake': Drawing by **Iribe**

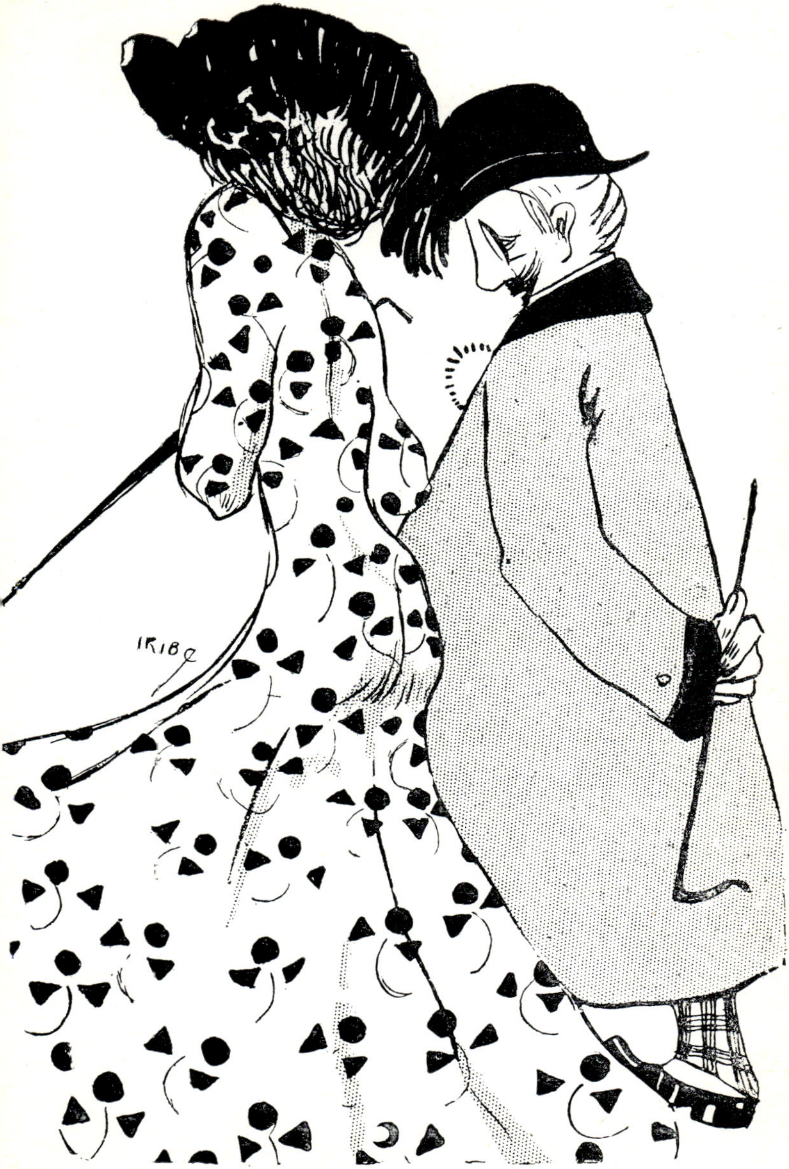
IRIBE

French caricature, c. 1900.

prime requirement. When the Philipon school was succeeded by the Caran d'Ache school a new kind of caricature came into being. The art of the *journalistes du crayon*, as Gill's biographer J. Valmy-Baysse called them, was giving place to a kind of caricature for caricature's sake.

Twentieth-century caricatures and cartoons

In the seventeenth century, Italy led the world in caricature, with Bernini and Ghezzi. In the eighteenth century, the initiative passed to England, with Hogarth, Rowlandson and Gillray. France took the lead in the nineteenth century, with the genius of the Daumier school and the founding of *Charivari*. But at the beginning of the twentieth century, the dominant country was Germany, which had Thomas Theodor Heine and Olaf Gulbransson of *Simplicissimus* in Munich and Arthur Johnson of *Kladderadatsch* in Berlin.

Olaf Gulbransson, a photograph portrait of the 1930s

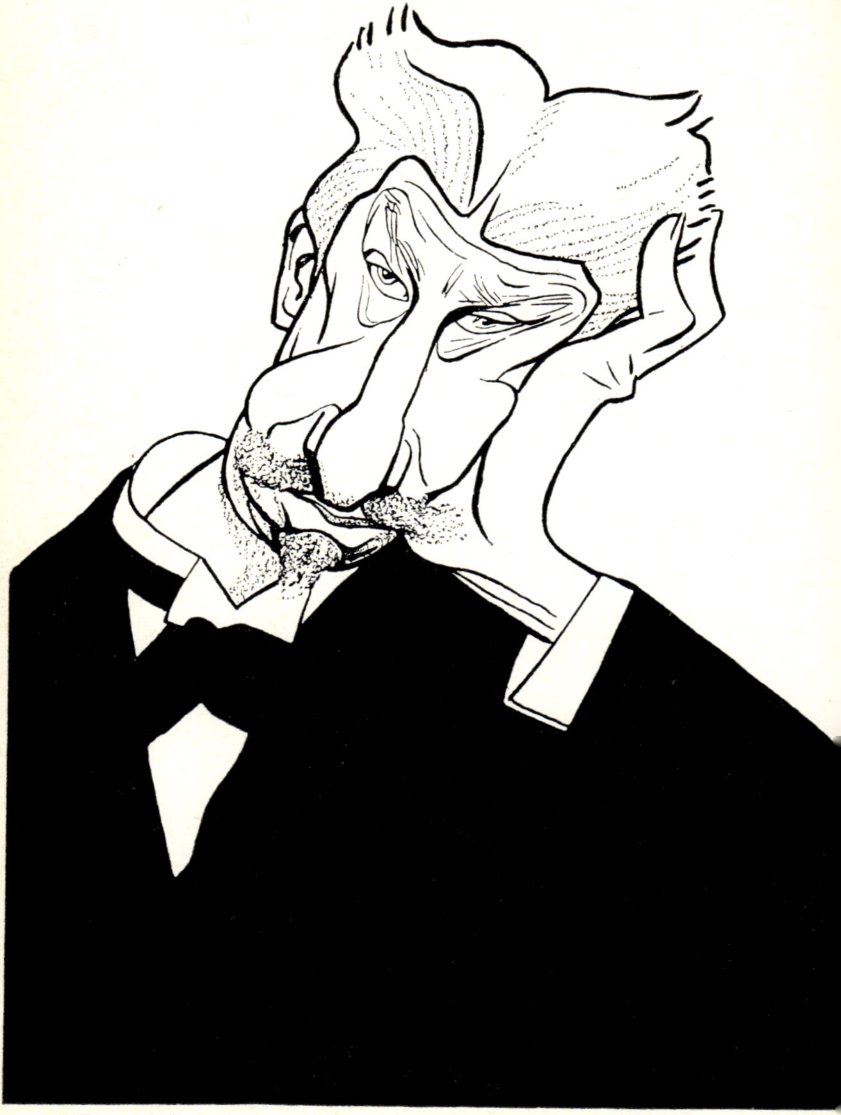

Simplicissimus was founded by Heine (1867–1948) in 1896, together with the publisher Albert Langen, who had come to Munich from the Rhineland. The title was derived from *Der Abentheurliche Simplicissimus Teutsch* (1669), a novel by Grimmelhausen. *Kladderadatsch*, as we have seen, was an earlier publication, now revitalized as a right-wing journal of political satire. These magazines commandeered the talents of the best cartoonists, who were not, as so often in England or America, hived off into daily newspaper work. The artists did not have to aim for the lowest common denominator; they were addressing a middle class who were trained, by the applied-art doctrines of Art Nouveau, to expect a degree of sophistication, if not of *avant-garde*, in the arts and crafts. Also, the two magazines used new colour processes far in advance of those available in the rest of Europe.

Artists such as Heine and Gulbransson took full advantage of this situation—the former in posters as well as cartoons. If one looks at the work Heine was producing in the late 1890s, one begins to wonder what was so revolutionary about the *Blaue Reiter* school founded, also in Munich, in 1911; and whether the basic precepts of cubism had not been anticipated years before Apollinaire began making them popular. By a kind of stream-lining, Heine invented, while Picasso and Braque were yet unknown, a style for the twentieth century. The intellectual calibre of the cartoons matched the writing in the magazine: Anatole France and Strindberg were among the writers, and *Simplicissimus* was almost the first to publish Thomas Mann, who later joined the editorial staff.

Gulbransson (1873–1958) was primarily a portrait caricaturist. Born in Oslo, he became a contributor to *Simplicissimus* in 1902. His technique is not unlike Max's: a Max less subtle but more virile, a Scandinavian Max happier with hand-woven ties and scarves and wooden houses than in straw hats, flannels and the sun of Rapallo. His style has cold deliberation and complete certainty. One of his best cartoons is of Delcassé riding a strutting cockerel at the time of the Agadir incident. Gulbransson was also one of the early mockers of Hitler. His style deteriorated, and his cartoon of 'Al Capone in Gaol' is more memorable for its caption

Olaf Gulbransson: Georg Brandes from *Simplicissimus*

than for its draughtsmanship : 'No wonder you've got an economic crisis when you fetter private enterprise with all your laws and restrictions.'

That was the kind of cartoon that would be unlikely to appear in *Kladderadatsch* : too left-wing. The chief caricaturist of the Berlin magazine was Arthur Johnson. He was born in America in 1874 of an American father and a German mother, and came to Germany from Cincinnati when his father was appointed American consul in Hamburg (1889). Johnson began as an academic painter. He studied at the Berlin Academy, won the Prix de Rome of the Prussian Academy, and was illustrated in *The Studio* and *Kunstwelt*. The grand manner infects most of his work : he is at his best when showing colossal figures of Mars or Militarism stumping across continents, or Peace with angel wings being picturesquely throttled by a giant in greaves and a fireman's helmet.

Simplicissimus took the lead in the propaganda battle against Great Britain and France in the First World War. British officers are usually represented as dour, drooping figures with wilting walrus moustaches. A caricature of 'English Civilization' by Bruno Paul (b.1874) gives us another chance to see ourselves as others saw us. The British riposte was Bruce Bairnsfather's 'Old Bill' ('If you knows of a better 'ole, go to it.') Bairnsfather was born in India, the son of a soldier. He attended the United Services College, Westward Ho, where Kipling had found the material for *Stalky & Co*. He joined the army as a second lieutenant, but soon left to study at John Hassall's art school in Kensington. On the outbreak of the First World War he went to France as a second lieutenant in his old regiment. In the trenches of Messines he began sketching again. Wounded at the second battle of Ypres, he spent his convalescence drawing. He was the first English artist to un-glorify war wholeheartedly. He tried to achieve in his cartoons something similar to what Siegfried Sassoon attempted in his poems. Critics in the House asked whether 'these vulgar caricatures of our heroes' should not be suppressed. But the heroes thought otherwise. They knew that Bairnsfather's view of the war was authentic. He even had letters from Germans saying 'We feel the same as you do'. The War Office evidently decided that if they could not beat

Bruno Paul: 'English Civilization' *Simplicissimus*

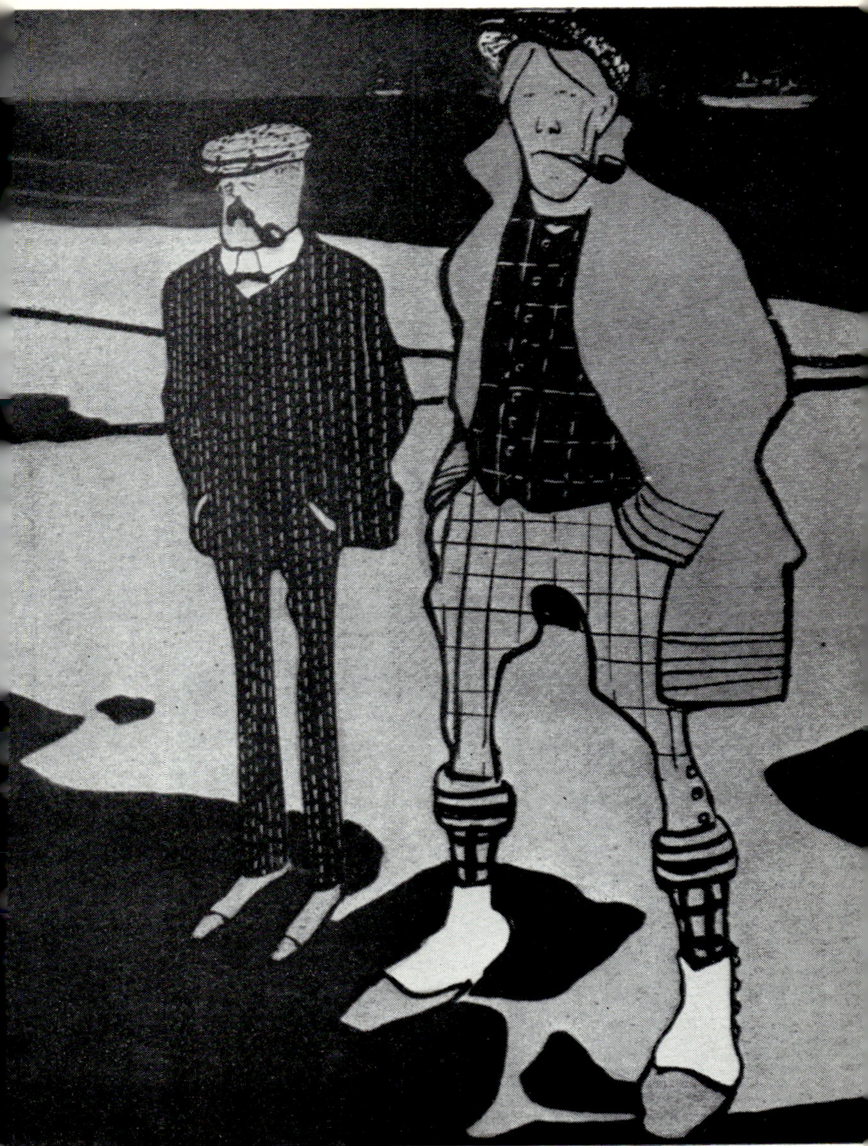

Low: 'How much will you give me not to kick your pants for, say, twenty-five years?' (1936)

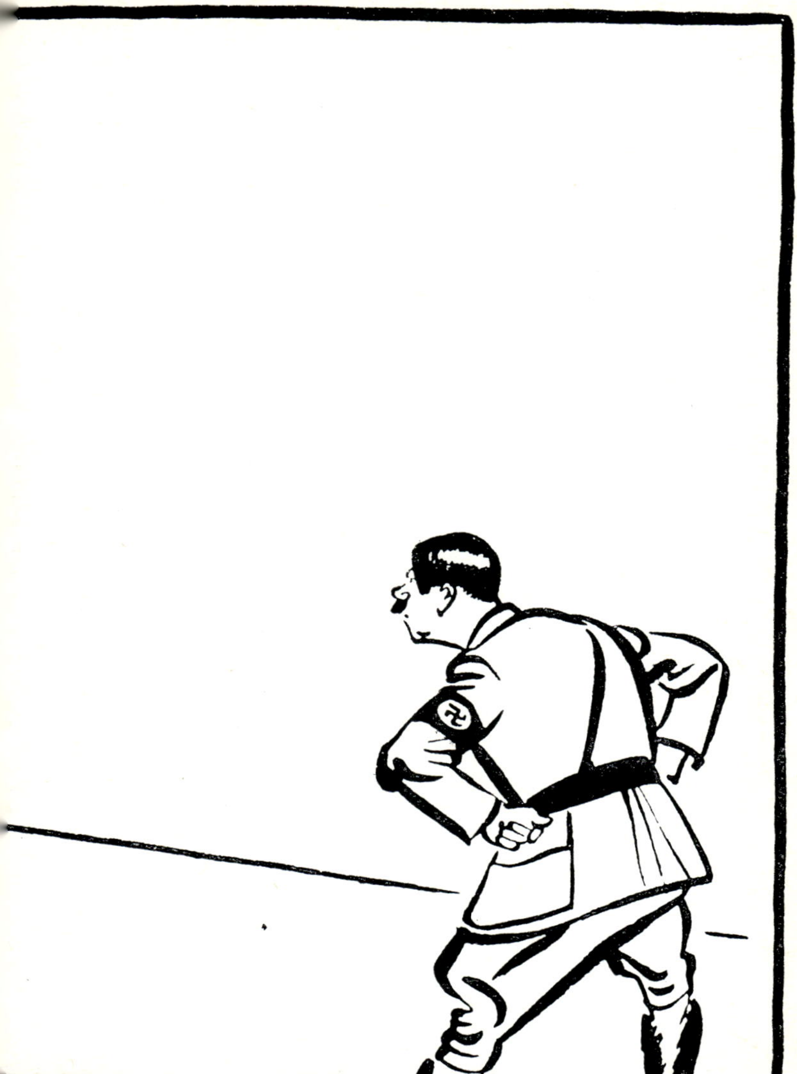

him, he should join them. He was placed in the Intelligence Department as Officer-Cartoonist. The French army borrowed him to create a Poilu Old Bill. Meanwhile Bert Thomas, a *Punch* cartoonist, had become a private in the Artists' Rifles. His 'Arf a Mo, Kaiser'—a grinning Tommy lighting his pipe and casually chatting to the German leader—collected £250,000 for the soldiers' tobacco fund. (He survived to mock Hitler too, with a sketch of Charlie Chaplin saying 'Copycat!')

America's principal war cartoonists were James Montgomery Flagg and Charles Dana Gibson (better known for inventing the 'Gibson Girl'). A Bureau of Cartoons was set up in December 1917, which in June 1918 was taken over by the Committee on Public Information. The Committee sent regular bulletins to every cartoonist, suggesting suitable subjects—popularize the draft, save food and fuel, buy Liberty Bonds. The most prophetic cartoon was Boardman Robinson's 1919 drawing of the Versailles Treaty being signed by a dead hand and nibbled by a mouse.

One of the great assets of the Allies was Louis Raemaekers, a Dutch cartoonist who drew for the Amsterdam *Telegraaf* before coming to England. Holland was neutral, and Raemaekers was wooed by the Germans; but the sight of the Belgian refugees who poured over the Dutch frontier convinced him that his place was with the Allies. In 1917 Lloyd George asked him to go to America to swing the Americans over to our side. This was something no British artist or politician could attempt. America was a neutral country and contained millions of Germans and people of German extraction. The British Navy had caused further ill feeling by searching American ships for contraband. Interference in the mails was another grievance. But now the sinking of the *Lusitania* had caused a shift in American sympathies. The impression Raemaekers made shifted them still further. Sir H. Perry Robinson, *The Times* War Correspondent, later said that he reckoned Raemaekers among the six men, including statesmen and army commanders, whose effort and influence had been most decisive in the war. Raemaeker's draughtsmanship is ragged and uninspired, but he often managed to make his cartoons impressive by using the figure of Christ, either on the cross or ascending prayerfully from bloodied fields. The kind of subject that really suited him was a good important death : when Clemenceau died in November 1929,

Miguel Covarrubias: C. Aubrey Smith and June Walker in 'The Bachelor Father' *The New Yorker*

Raemaekers drew the old statesman shambling off into eternity waving his cane and gloves at cohorts of silent troops: 'La Dernière Marche'.

The early twentieth century saw the rise of the newspaper cartoonist. Through the practice of syndication—the use of one drawing by several papers—the cartoonist could reach an audience of millions. In America the newspaper cartoon first became a force through Walt McDougall's satire in the *New York World* at the end of the presidential campaign in 1884. But it was not until the late '90s that cartoons became a regular feature in the American daily papers, with artists such as Leon Barritt, Valerian Gribayedoff, C. G. Bush and Van Sant. Cartoonists used to the easy pace of magazine work, found the change difficult. As McDougall said, most of them 'were geared too low for the fast-moving stuff that hopped circulations up', while others 'were too high-hat and artistic for the class to which newspapers appeal'. There were raids and counter-raids by newspaper owners such as William Randolph Hearst and Joseph Pulitzer for the services of the best cartoonists, while English newspapers too began to hire them. David Low was taken on by *The Star* in 1919. Sidney Strube joined the *Daily Express* and Will Dyson the *Daily Herald*.

Low (1891–1963) was a New Zealander who came to England after the First World War. His cartoon style, which combined crudeness with accuracy, has been overpraised in England because of the natural affection for an artist who led anti-Hitler propaganda. Low joined the *Evening Standard* in 1927, and his attacks on Hitler began in 1933. At first this attitude provoked some hostility. One of his critics told him he was so Low he would have to go to hell in a balloon. When he called his dog Mussolini, he was visited by an excited Italian who had come to express the anguish of the entire Italian people at this sacrilege. Low invented Colonel Blimp and his proletarian counterpart, the TUC carthorse. His satire, like Gillray's, was directed at all parties, and Winston Churchill, smarting under one of his sallies, called him a 'green-eyed Antipodean rebel'.

'Strube', of the *Daily Express*, who popularized the ineffectual 'little man' in cartoons, was another product of the Hassall art school. His first work was for the *Conservative and Unionist* (later published as *Our Flag*) just before the General Election of 1910. Will Dyson was an infinitely better draughtsman than either Low or Strube, and possessed a caustic wit comparable at times with that of Max. The devil crouches above the skyscrapers of New York and peers down : 'Well, well, well ; one lives and learns'. Noël Coward and Epstein are looking at a piece of Epstein's sculpture. 'Of course, Mr Epstein,' says Coward, 'I speak only as a layman —for the moment I have done no sculpture'. A 'modern' artist, surrounded by his chaotic works, says : 'Sometimes I feel like chucking it all and going in for Art !' Dr Freud reproves a maiden who will not understand that prudish thoughts spring from lewd desires : 'Naughty, naughty ; who's been thinking pure thoughts again ?' And 'Count Tolstoy suspecting sensuality in the Heavenly choir' is pure Max. Dyson's danger was a too great subtlety, an irony above his readers' heads.

Magazines of the 1920s responded to the post-war mood of gaiety at all costs. The *New Yorker* (started in 1925) had Peter Arno baiting the 'booboisie', the *roués* of Ralph Barton (1891– 1931), the poached-eyed people of Rea Irvin, the anti-business cartoons of Gluyas Williams and Ellison Hoover, and the *avant- garde* works of the Mexican Miguel Covarrubias (1904–57), whose caricatures are the nearest approach to cubism that any caricaturist has felt it possible to attempt, consistent with getting a likeness.

Of the really 'twentyish' caricaturists, the most accomplished were Nerman, whose laconic sketch of Delysia is an Art Deco masterwork ; Edmond Dulac, who sometimes took time off from his jewelled book illustration to pen a precise caricature, such as his wicked cameo of George Moore ; Powys Evans who as 'Quiz' drew distorted heads of twenties' notabilities like Roger Fry ; and Rex Whistler, who painted a 'typical Guards officer' for the Welsh Guards, in which he served, the voluptuous vision of the Regent unveiling the spirit of Brighton, in the Brighton Pavilion, and a caricature, here published for the first time, of Lieutenant- Colonel Andrew Graham, now Wine Correspondent of *The Times*.

Situation comedy was the new fashion. The old political clichés of the cartoonist—the precipice labelled 'Crisis', the octopus labelled 'Protection', the tightrope labelled 'Elections', gave place to a new set of situation clichés : the magic carpet, the psy- chiatrist's couch, the cannibal's cooking pot, the drunken husband and rolling-pin reception, the men from Mars ('Take me to your

Nerman: caricature of Delysia *The Tatler*

Edmond Dulac: George Moore

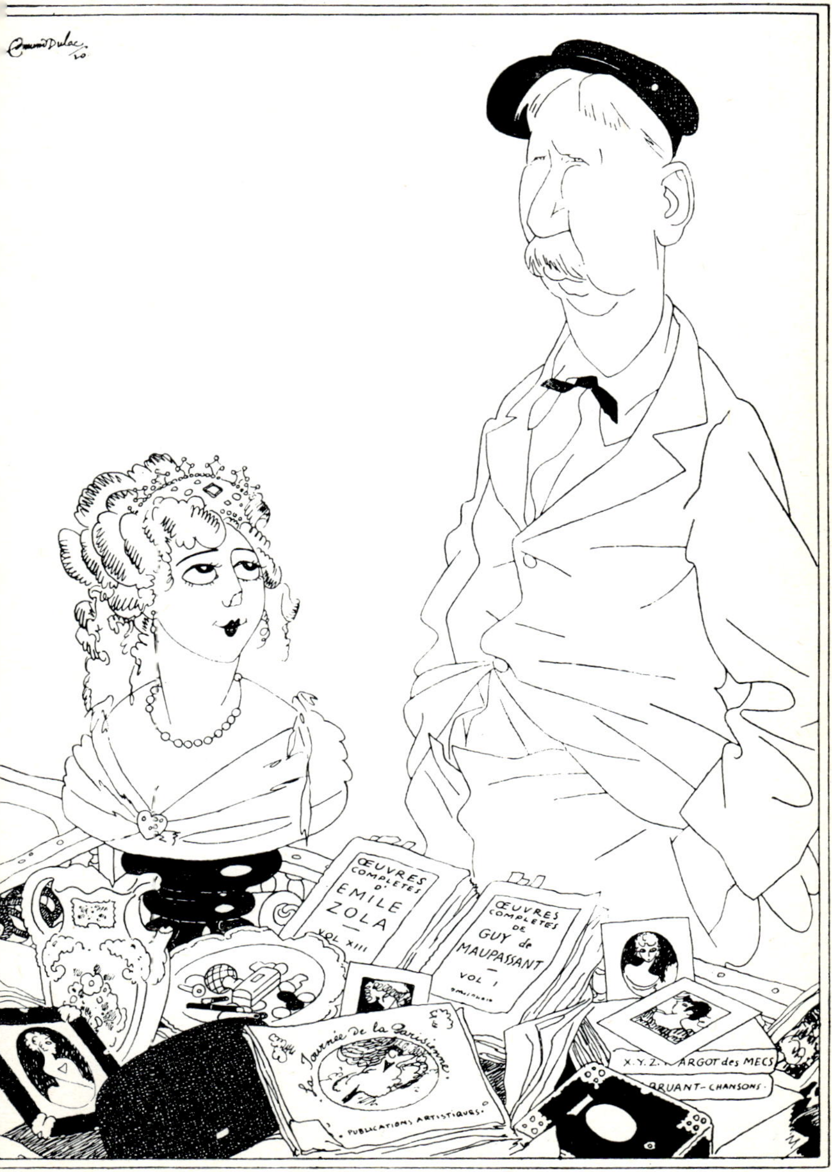

Edmund Dulac 20
ŒUVRES COMPLETES D' EMILE ZOLA
VOL XIII
ŒUVRES COMPLETES DE GUY de MAUPASSANT
VOL I
La Journée de la Parisienne
PUBLICATIONS ARTISTIQUES
X.Y.Z.
ARGOT des MECS

Caricature of Roger Fry by **'Quiz'** (Powys Evans)

'A f ne pair of Charlies' by **Rex Whistler,** 1940. (The central figure is Lieutenant-Colonel Andrew Graham, now Wine Correspondent of *The Times*) *By courtesy of Laurence Whistler, Esq., and of Lieutenant-Colonel Graham*

lieder' says a green-faced monster to Franz Schubert) or, the most overworked of all, the desert island castaways (the best of which was published by *Punch* after two films had been made about Oscar Wilde's trials. One castaway to the other: 'I've just had a good idea. When we get back, I'm going to make a film about the trials of Oscar Wilde.')

Punch had two masters of situation comedy, H. M. Bateman (1887–1970), and 'Pont' (Graham Laidler, 1908–40). (Both have recently been the subjects of good biographies, by respectively, Michael Bateman (no relation) and Bernard Hollowood, a former Editor of *Punch*.) Bateman invented the 'Odd man out' joke. Eyes bulge and hands are raised in horror at 'The man who asked whether the meat [at Simpson's in the Strand] was English or foreign'; 'the Guest who wanted to kiss the bride'; 'The curate who saw red'. In 'Edgar Wallace Entertains', he showed a drawing room with dagoes knifing each other while a police sergeant sits impassively in the foreground. His portrayal of artists and writers in their own manner was never more piquant than in the vision of Gauguin painting dusky beauties in Mother Hubbards, on a minute island. Pont's style was less demonstrative, but was well adapted to such subjects as 'The British Character' on which he drew a series in the 1930s: 'Importance of Not being an alien'; 'The gift of water colours'; 'Absolute indispensability of bacon and egg for breakfast'. At times he could break away from his usual temperate style in flights of crazy surrealism, as in *The People Behind*, one of his series of 'Popular Misconceptions': a small boy in church has been told it is rude to look round, and imagines behind him a pewful of monsters—a horned god with a loaf of bread on his head, a man with his hair on end, others with asses ears and a top hat with a marmoset peering over the crown.

Ernest H. Shepard (b. 1879) was also working for *Punch* at this time, in the same restrained and wholly delightful style in which he had illustrated the Pooh Bear stories. He was an artist who found it difficult, or perhaps unnecessary, to adapt his style or conventions as time passed; in the 1950s he was still drawing schoolboys in the boots and long knickerbockers worn by Edwardian boys. He is drawing still, at 90. In 1968 one of his Pooh drawings, owned by the Prince of Pudukota, fetched £1200 in a Sotheby's sale. Punch published a parody of A. A. Milne on this event, headed by a

H. M. Bateman, 'The man who asked whether the meat [at Simpson's in the Strand] was English or foreign' *Simpson's in the Strand*

H. M. Bateman: 'Gauguin Chez Lui' *I. R. D. Byfield, Esq.*

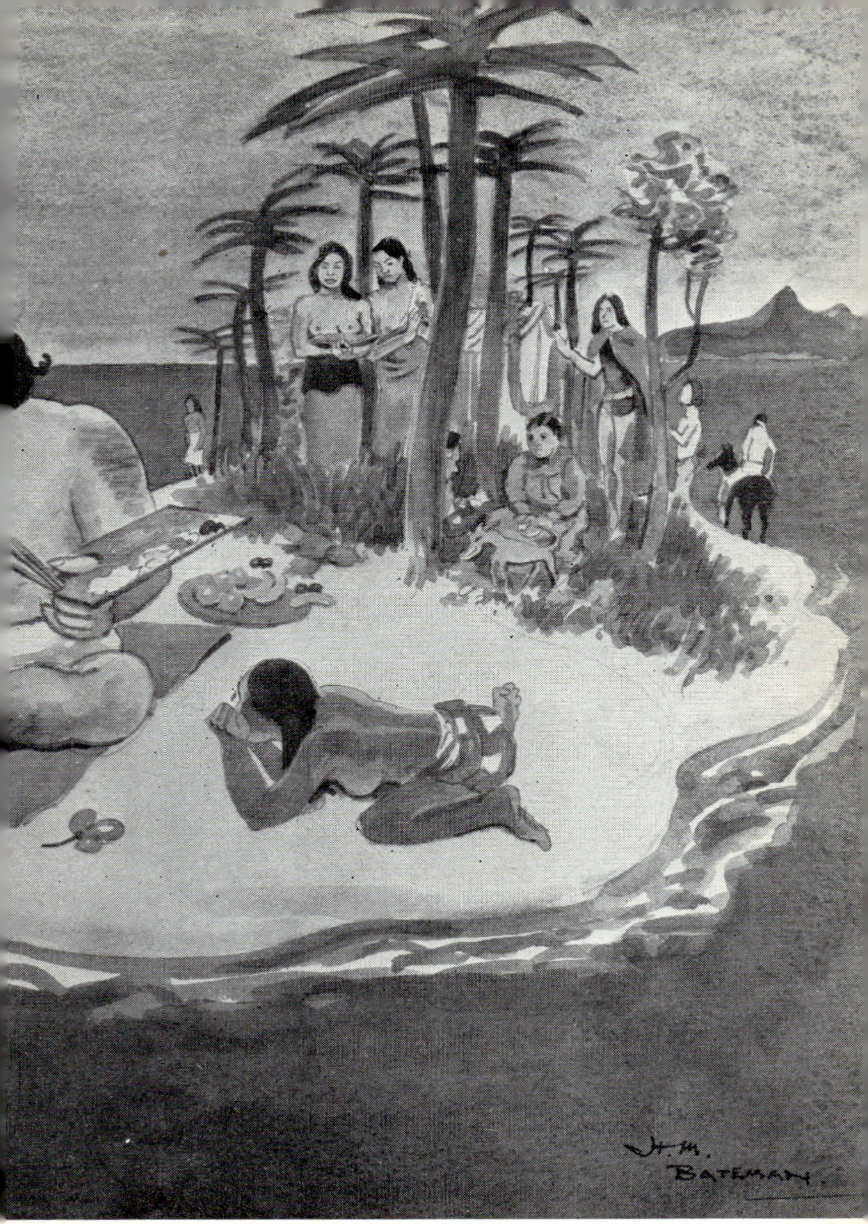
H.M. BATEMAN.

Hewison parody of a Shepard drawing—showing a sketch of Eyore being auctioned by Christopher Robin. It began:

Pooh was humming a Good Hum, Such as is Hummed Boastfully to Others.

> Sotheby, Botheby,
> Tiddeley-pom
> The sketch of our picnic
> Has sold for a bomb.

Kenneth Bird ('Fougasse'—he chose the pseudonym to avoid confusion with another *Punch* artist, W. Bird) contributed his first cartoon to *Punch* in 1916. It was called 'War's Brutalizing Influence' and showed how a fashion-plate young subaltern was converted into a tough pipe-smoking veteran. But it was the Second World War that made him famous, with his 'Careless Talk Costs Lives' drawings of Nazi leaders sitting in London buses or materializing from behind telephone kiosks. He had become art editor of *Punch* in 1937. 'Fougasse' was another ex-pupil of Hassall, but had independently developed his style of little stickmen, which lent itself to social comedies, especially those requiring crowd scenes, like the private view at an art gallery.

Victor Weisz ('Vicky', 1913–1968) was another cartoonist who won great popularity by his wartime contributions, in this case to the *News Chronicle*. (He later joined the *Daily Mirror* and, in 1958, the *Evening Standard*.) He had been born a Hungarian citizen in Berlin, where he studied art. At fourteen, his father's death forced him to start selling caricatures. The rise of Nazism turned him to political cartoons in 1929; but it is alleged that when he arrived in England in 1935, the only English politicians he had heard of were Chamberlain, Churchill and Baldwin. Vicky's style is similar to Low's—brusque, inelegant, but adaptable and workmanlike.

George Grosz (1893–1959), who had joined the Dadaist movement soon after its foundation in 1916, showed how anti-Nazi cartoons could also be works of art. Only John Heartfield (b.1891), with his brilliant montage techniques, conveyed more directly the malevolence of Nazism. The most effective Russian anti-Nazi cartoonist was Kukrinski, who favoured caustic allegories.

German propaganda against Great Britain is seen at its most virulent in *Signal*, the German propaganda magazine issued in occupied countries such as France. Here the German idea of a

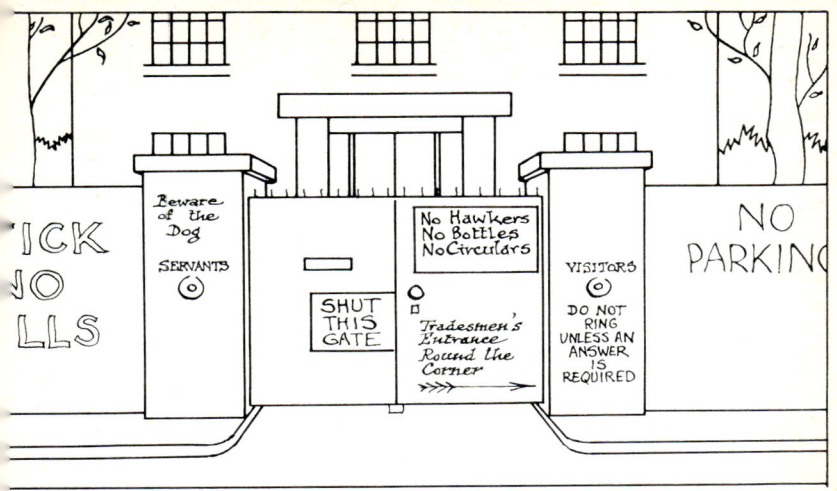

'Fougasse' (Kenneth Bird) : The Changing Face of Britain ; Englishman's House
Fine Art Society Ltd

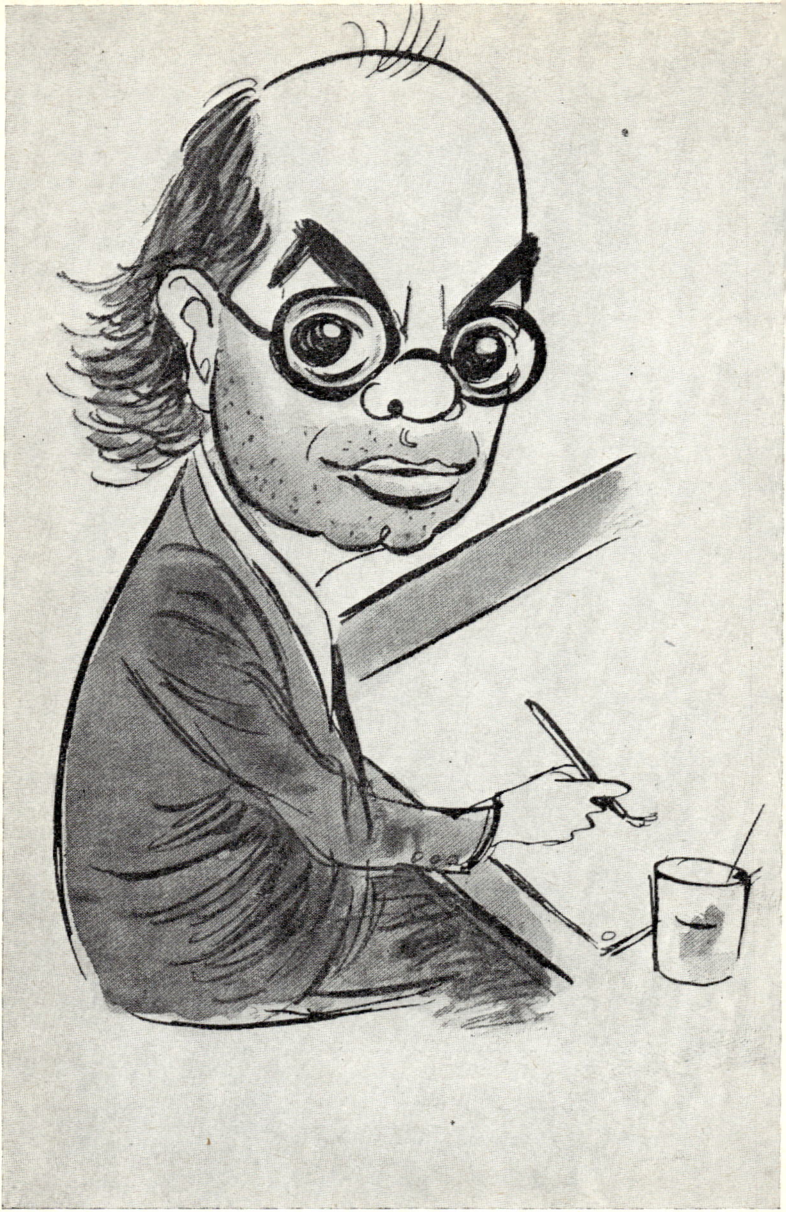

Kukrinski: a caricature of Hitler: he is being painted by Goebbels

A self-portrait by **Vicky** (Victor Weisz)

George Grosz: the Republican President Ebert

typical Englishman is represented as a sneering, monocled toff
rearranging Europe, jigsaw-fashion, into the shape of Britain.

Punch has had some admirable artists since the war. Ronald
Searle (b.1920) who had been taken prisoner by the Japanese,
and in 1946 published a book of harrowing drawings of his
experiences, began contributing to *Punch* in 1949 and joined the
staff in 1956. He is best known for the fiendish schoolgirls of
St Trinian's ('Hands up the girl who burnt down the east wing last
night'). Rowland Emett (b.1906) had been a war draughtsman in
the development of jet engines. He had made his first contribution

134

Anonymous caricature of Neville Chamberlain

to *Punch* in 1939. His speciality was wispy locomotives and strange gadgets—we might call such things 'Emett contraptions' if Heath Robinson had not pioneered them. In 1951 he designed a full scale working model of the 'Far Tottering and Oyster Creek Railway' to carry passengers in the Battersea pleasure gardens, London, during the Festival of Britain. Gerard Hoffnung (1925–59) created musical fantasies, not only in his *Punch* cartoons, but also in absurd concerts for vacuum cleaners (a genuine 'Hoover' had the cachet of a Stradivarius) at the Royal Festival Hall, where a memorial concert was also held for him in 1960. 'Anton' (Antonia

135

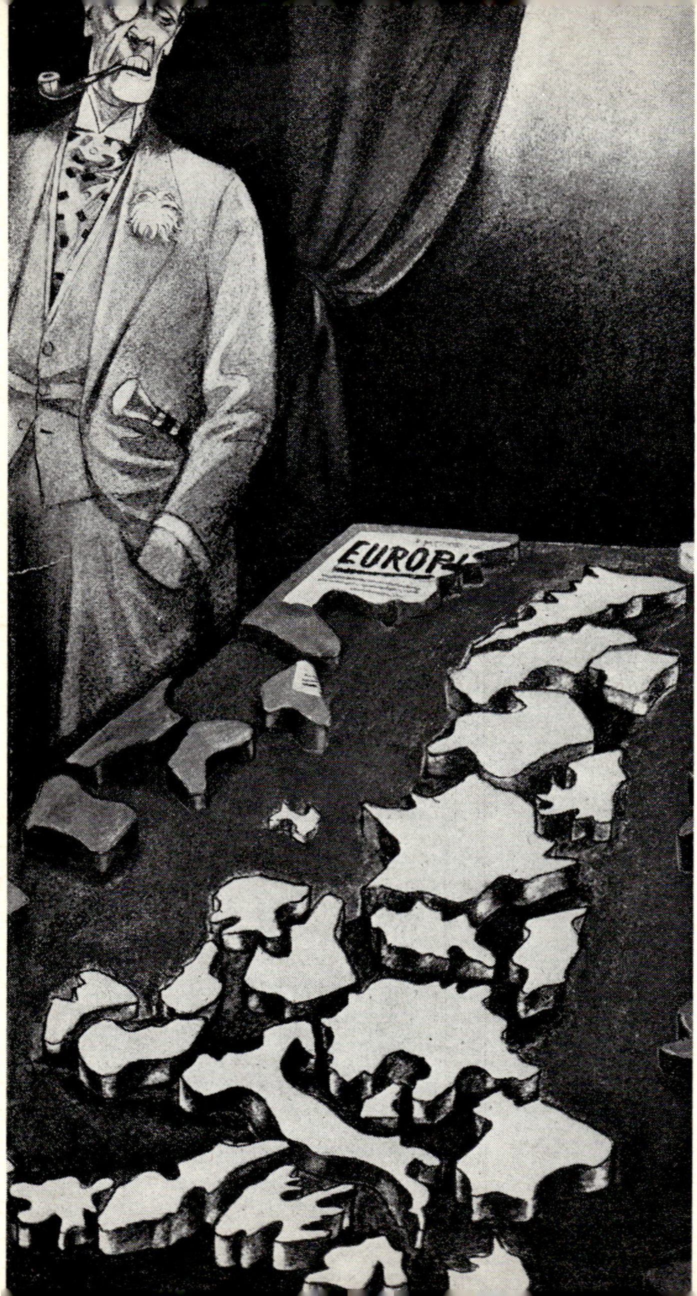
EUROP

Rowland Emett: 'Despite a severe depletion of rolling stock . . .'
Annabel's Club

'The English Europe-puzzle': from *Signal*, the German propaganda magazine issued in occupied France, December 1940

Class warfare in schooling : Public schoolboy by **Leslie Illingworth** (*Daily Mail*, 6 September 1961).

Yeoman, b.1914, and H. Underwood Thompson, b.1910) played situation games with elegant upper-middle-class people. Thelwell's main stock-in-trade has been horsey little girls of the kind immortalized in Sir John Betjeman's poem 'It's aw'flly bad luck on Diana . . .' but in his full colour pages he has satirized the modern English scene more widely. When I won a *Punch* competition in 1959, the good old days when they gave original cartoons as prizes, I chose Thelwell's 'The age-old custom of beating the balm-cake at Abbots Dawdling'—a pullulating drawing which shows how a folk custom is vulgarized for American
138

PLblic and Grammar school boys by **Horner** (*New Statesman*, 27 May 1966) ;
Secondary modern schoolboy by **Haro** (*Daily Mail*, 7 December 1963).

tourist consumption, with leggy drum majorettes, platoons of
photographers, and neon signs indicating antique shops and Olde
Tea Rooms. Among so many who favoured the Searle–Thelwell
manner of fuzzy, frisky lines, Nicolas Bentley (who also 'drew the
pictures' for so many books) preserved a calm, undeviating clarity
of line. His miniature drawing of Sir Kenneth (now Lord) Clark is
every bit as revealing as Ronald Searle's more ambitious caricature
portraits of Bertrand Russell and T. S. Eliot.

Another minor master of the clear, cool line is Osbert Lancaster
(b.1908) who drew his first 'little cartoon' in Tom Driberg's

column in the *Daily Express* in 1939. Lord and Lady Littlehampton update very well, from jokes about test-tube babies ('I know for a fact, my dear, that she comes from one of the oldest and most illustrious test-tubes in Europe') to the most deflating of all comments on man's first landing on the moon (the two stargazers look up at a moon just like a Coca-Cola bottle top, complete with trade-name. 'I think they've arrived, darling'.). Mr Lancaster's books of architectural parody combine fine draughtsmanship and a wide knowledge of architecture (at one time he worked for the *Architectural Review*). Mr Lancaster provides cartoons of the aristocracy for the front page of the *Daily Express*; inside, Giles offers working-class comedy. His best-loved creation is Grandma, with her Noah's Ark hat, pipe and betting slips. Carl Ronald Giles (b.1916) joined the *Daily Express* in 1942, having previously worked for Alexander Korda and *Reynolds News*, and went as a War Correspondent with the Second Army to France, Belgium, Holland and Germany. Other good newspaper cartoonists working now are Illingworth, Emmwood, Cummings—and Haro, whose economy of line is sometimes so drastic that one scarcely has enough evidence to decide whether he is a good draughtsman or not.

The supremacy of *Punch* in English visual humour, which had lasted for more than a century, was challenged in the early 1960s by the publication of a new magazine, *Private Eye*. A forerunner of the 'satire movement'—'Beyond the Fringe', 'That Was the Week That Was', 'Not so much a Programme', the French magazine *Hara-kiri*, the 'Rowan and Martin Laugh-In'—it began as a kind of sequel to the Oxford undergraduate magazine *Mesopotamia*, and took over its main cartoonist, William Rushton, who has a fine spiky style, a good line in bottle-nosed club bores, and an endearing habit of giving his characters hooves instead of feet. It also adopted the Horlicks advertisement technique of superimposing voice balloons on photographs. *Private Eye*'s most valuable discovery was Gerald Scarfe who brought to the art of caricature well assimilated modern influences. In 1950, Milton Shulman in *How to be a Celebrity* (a collection of essays on notables of the time) wrote:

Some potential victims give Vicky a little help by cultivating habits or acquiring idiosyncrasies. Truman, fortunately, wears

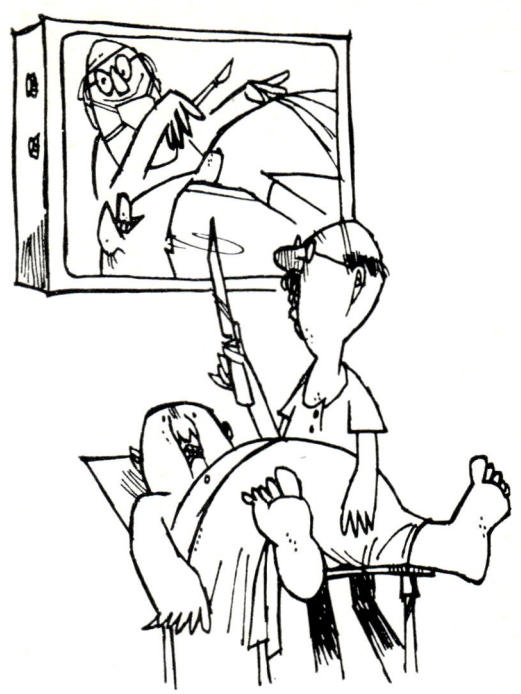

Cartoon by **Rushton** of do-it-yourself surgery, *Private Eye*, 30 November 1962

Cn pages 142 and 143
William Rushton and friend, 1969 *Photograph by Malcolm Lewis*

glasses, Baldwin smoked a pipe and Chamberlain carried an umbrella. Harold Wilson, President of the Board of Trade, is practically hopeless from a cartoonist's point of view. There is nothing in his face that is remotely abnormal. 'I wish he'd grow a beard or something,' Vicky sighed. And then he added a remark which showed how low Wilson had really sunk in the artistic scheme of things. 'I still have to stick a label on him', he said, as if confessing some secret crime.

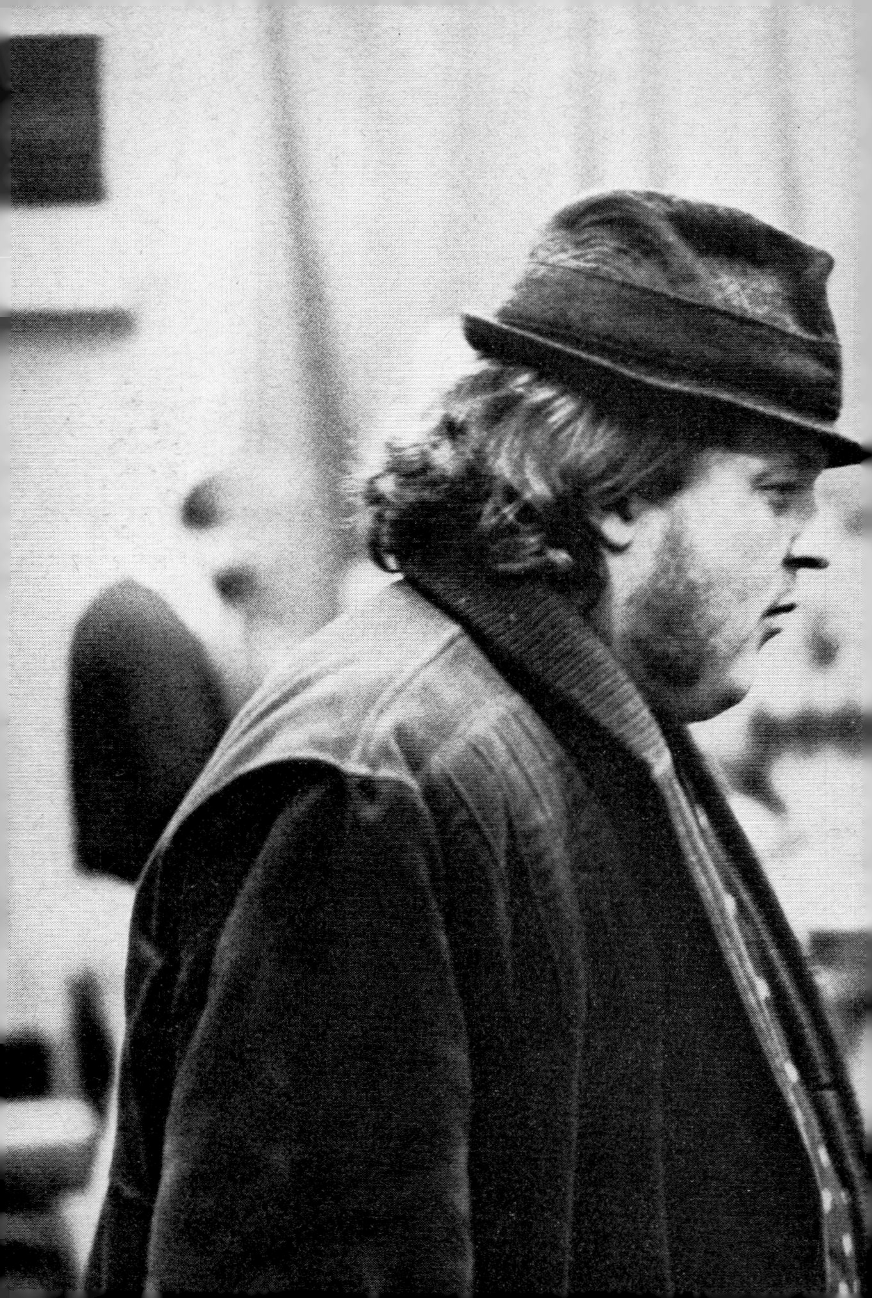

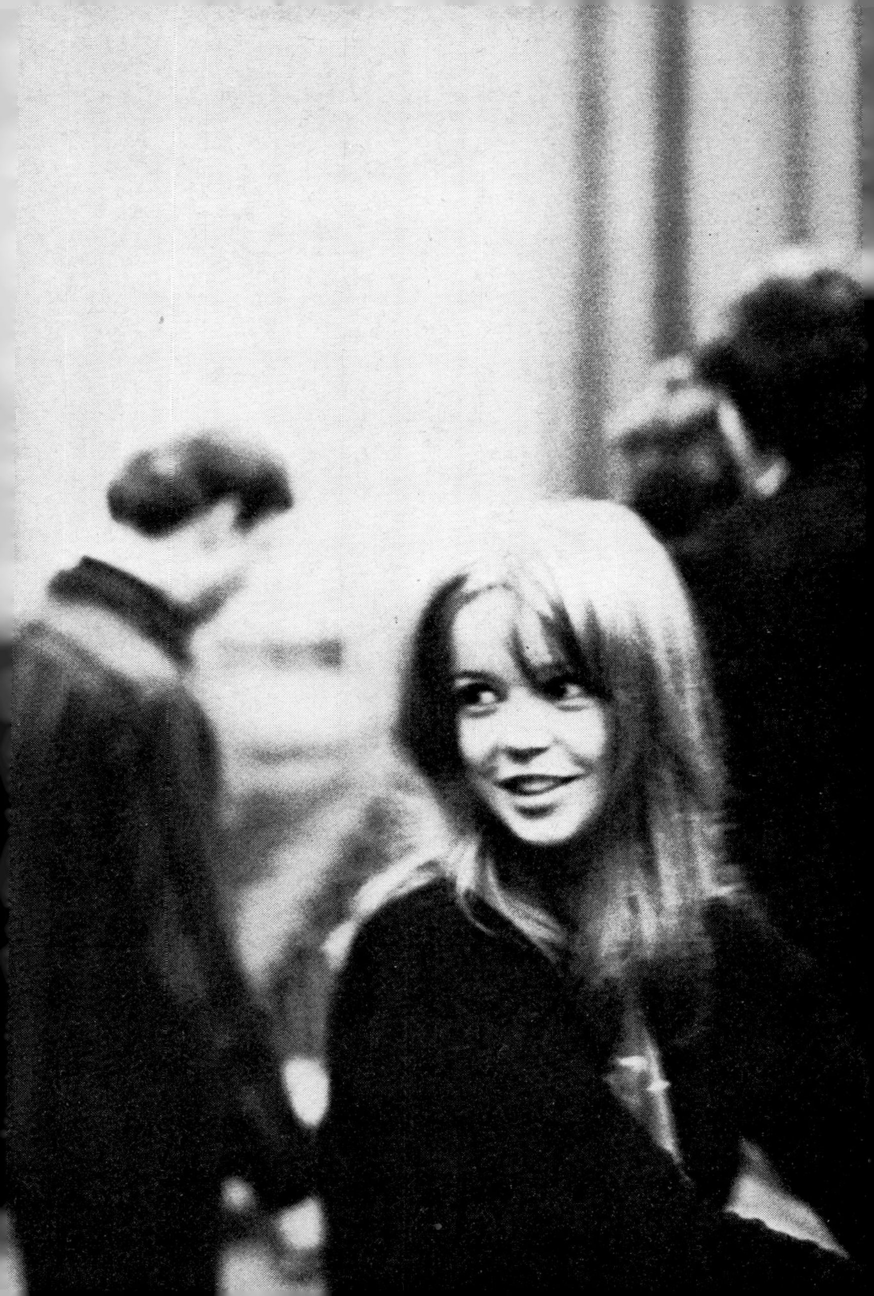

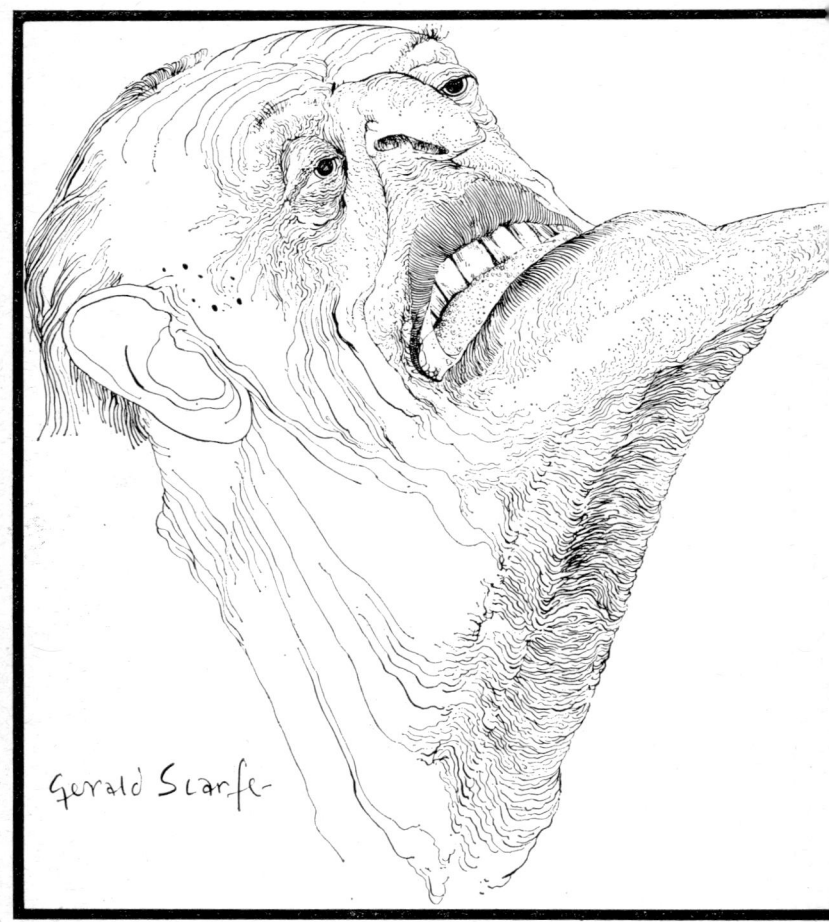

Somerset Maugham, as seen by **Scarfe** in 1967 and

Scarfe has never had to stick a label on anyone. He can convey the expression of a man's hair. His Prime Minister Wilson is toothily 'sincere' and disingenuous. His Edward Heath has a vast smile-mask to hitch up over his natural pout. His Somerset Maugham is dissolving in cynical wrinkles : an interesting contrast with Covar-

Miguel Covarrubias in 1927

rubias's caricature of Maugham in 1927, in which only the cast of the head is the same.

'Larry' and Bill Tidey, who both have a notional, doodling style of draughtsmanship, a controlled haphazardness, draw for both *Punch* and *Private Eye*. Larry's *forte* is the working-class Mum and

145

"We'll have to wait for the photo, but I made it .

Bill Tidey: *Private Eye*, 10 October 1969

Dad: he is especially happy in summer, when he can send them off to a Seaview Boarding House. Tidey's humour is further off-beat, and to me he is the funniest cartoonist working today. There is a zany inexplicability in the situations his rambling pen presents: 'I assure you, Major, my wife is always being mistaken for a Sherpa.' I recently saw a television programme about him, in which we saw William Davis, the present Editor of *Punch*, rejecting

s Tanya of Trachtenburg by a neck!"

one of his drawings because he thought it too recondite for his readers. I thought it one of Tidey's best: the Ruritanian state funeral, with a train of mourners and the caption: 'This could mean war. It was the Archduke Frederick's turn to carry the spare wheel.' Another of Tidey's royal funeral cartoons is illustrated here.

Tidey must have learnt a lot from two of the best American cartoonists of the last 20 years, James Thurber (1894–1961) and

Bill Tidey: 'Building loans are a bit tight, Eminence. How many nuns were you thinking of walling up?' *Private Eye*, 10 October 1969

Charles Addams (b.1912). Thurber joined the *New Yorker* as Managing Editor in 1927. He wrote and illustrated his first book, *Is Sex Necessary?* in collaboration with E. B. White of the New Yorker staff, before any of his drawings had been reproduced in the magazine. His cartoons first appeared there in 1930. He had a genius for way-out situation comedies: for example, a couple in bed with a seal peering mournfully over the headboard so we can see it but they can't—'All right, have it your own way, you heard a seal bark!' His shapeless, hippo-like animals are a marvel of expressive undraughtsmanship. Charles Addams's death-enhancing cartoons of the ghoulish Munster family are another

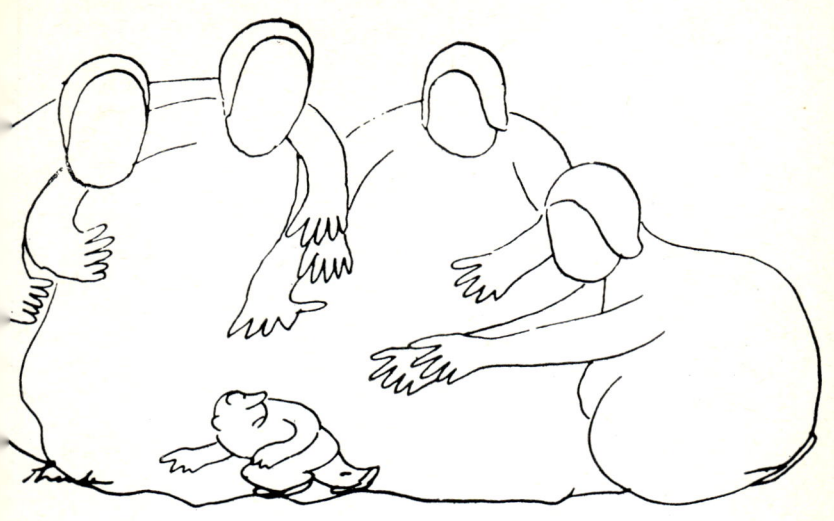

James Thurber: illustration to his book *Credos and Curios* (1962)

innovation in situation jokes. While Thurber's cartoons take commonplace suburban reality (like the couple's bedroom) and set off its absurdity (by adding the seal), Addams's drawings require that we should accept from the start a completely unconvincing world of Frankenstein butlers, Munch-faced châtelaines, and evil turreted manses. Within this sinister framework he sets the commonplaces of life and thus invests them with absurdity. The lady of the house looks up startled as the door creaks open. 'Oh, it's only you', she says in relief, as the horrific swaying Boris Karloff servant looms in the door. The Munsters have fastened on the American consciousness like domesticated vampire bats.

Saul Steinberg is another *New Yorker* contributor whose cartoons have had an international influence. Born at Ramnic Sarat, Rumania, in 1914, he studied psychology and sociology at Bucharest University. He joined the *New Yorker* staff in 1941. His language of visual puns and conundrums is austere and intellectual, and Professor Gombrich is among those who have written about him as a significant twentieth-century artist.

But the main contribution of America to the twentieth-century cartoon is the less sophisticated one of comic strips. The genre had been pioneered by Wilhelm Busch in *Max und Moritz* (Rudoph Dirks based his Katzenjammer Kids, which first appeared in 1897, on Busch.) Rodolphe Töpffer (1799–1846) had also drawn comic sequences, as had Caran d'Ache. But the widespread popularity of the comic strip really began in 1896, with the publication of Richard F. Outcault's 'Yellow Kid' in the *New York World* Sunday supplement. Outcault was promptly enticed over to the *New York Journal* by Hearst. Then Pulitzer's *World* bought him back again. This farce of bids and counter-bids led to the phrase 'Yellow Journalism'. The comic sequence was taken up in *Ally Sloper's Half-Holiday*. Lord Northcliffe's *Comic Cuts*, for children, first appeared in 1890, and lasted for 60 years. The first 'Teddy Tail' sequence appeared in the *Daily Mail* in 1915. Rupert Bear's adventures began in the *Daily Express* in 1920. Then Northcliffe had the bright idea that what appealed to children could be adapted for adults too: 'Pop' by Millar Watt (Gordon Hogg after 1948) began in the *Daily Sketch* in 1921. 'Dot and Carrie', drawn by J. K. Horrabin, was introduced in *The Star* in 1923. The adorable 'Jane' arrived in the *Daily Mirror* in 1932 as 'The Diary of a Bright Young Thing'. She was drawn by Norman Pett (Mike Hubbard took over in 1947). The best of the more recent comic strips have been 'Flook' in the *Daily Mail*, drawn by 'Trog' (Humphrey Lyttleton, and later George Melly wrote the excellent social-satire captions) and 'Bristow' in the *Evening Standard* by Frank Dickens. Bristow is Strube's 'little man', triumphantly *redivivus*. His domineering boss, Fudge, his *princesse lointaine*, Miss Pretty of Kleenaphone, and his sensational but uncompleted novel *Living Death in the Buying Department* are an only slightly heightened version of the reality his commuter audience live and love.

Charles Addams: 'I know, but I don't go in unless he buzzes.'

BRISTOW *BY FRANK DICKENS*

WITH A *SENSE OF HUMOUR* AS DEVELOPED AS MINE IT IS DIFFICULT TO TAKE *WORK* SERIOUSLY...

TO ME IT IS JUST AMUSING WAY OF PASSING THE TIM

'Bristow' by **Frank Dickens**: a typical episode

FLOOK — *The Diabolical Deb.*

JEREMY, ARE YOU COMING OR NOT?

'E WAS SAYIN' *'SEE YER AROUND'* TO ME IF YOU MUST KNOW

WELL, HE'D BETTER CHANGE IT TO *'GOODB* I SHALL MAKE QUITE SURE YOU GET ASKED TO NOTHING. I CAN'T THINK WHAT LADY FFOLLY WAS...

'Flook' by **'Trog'**: note the classic representation of the **chinless wonder** and the **chinful wonderess**

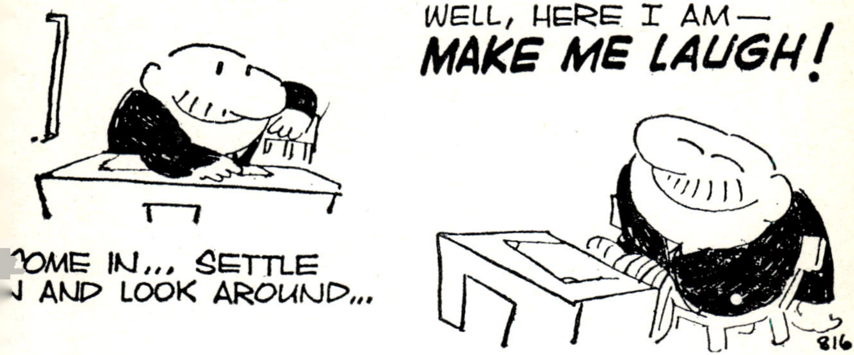
OME IN,,, SETTLE
N AND LOOK AROUND...
WELL, HERE I AM—
MAKE ME LAUGH!
816

by Trog

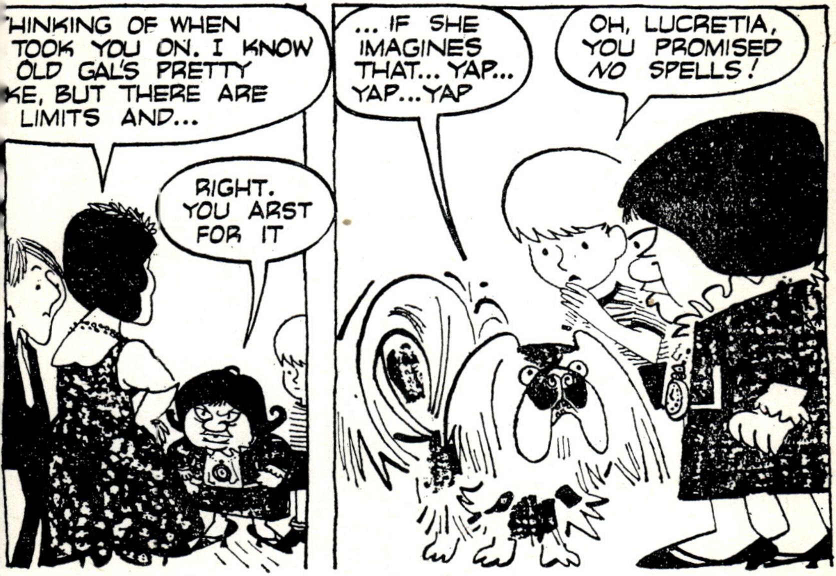
HINKING OF WHEN TOOK YOU ON. I KNOW OLD GAL'S PRETTY KE, BUT THERE ARE LIMITS AND...
RIGHT. YOU ARST FOR IT
... IF SHE IMAGINES THAT... YAP... YAP... YAP
OH, LUCRETIA, YOU PROMISED NO SPELLS!

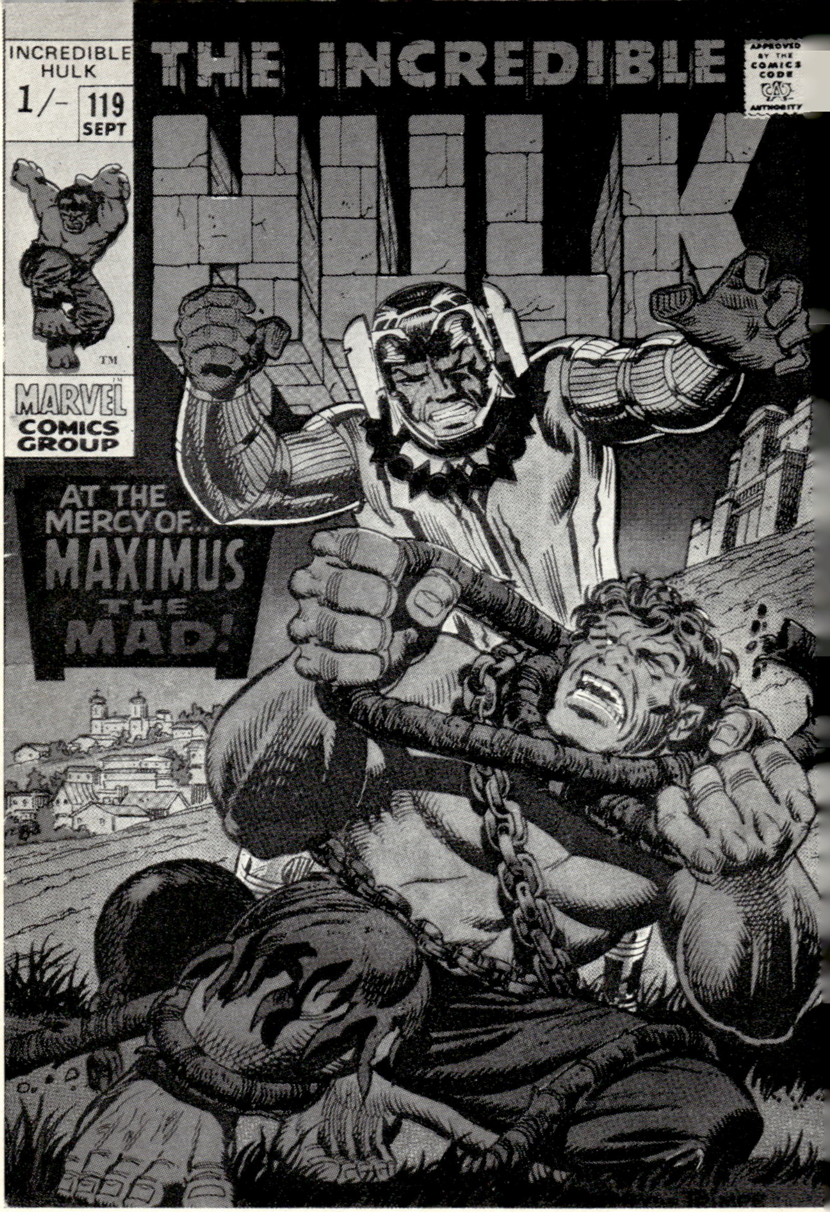
INCREDIBLE HULK
1/-
119
SEPT
THE INCREDIBLE
HULK
APPROVED BY THE COMICS CODE AUTHORITY
MARVEL COMICS GROUP
AT THE MERCY OF... MAXIMUS THE MAD!

In its most advanced pictorial form—in American comics such as *Superman, Batman* and *Captain Marvel,* and in 'horror comics' such as *Hulk*—the comic strip has become part of the prevailing High Kitsch, an inspiration for Roy Lichtenstein, who is concerned to incorporate into his art 'the most brazen and threatening characteristics of our culture, things we hate, but which are also powerful in their impingement on us'. The exhibition of Lichtenstein's comic-strip works at the Tate Gallery in 1968 was the apotheosis of the cartoonist.

Apotheosis, but not supreme achievement. For if this book—a thumbnail sketch of thumbnail sketches—proves anything, it is that one must not look for a 'development' or 'progress' in this art. There is no 'great tradition' of the kind Dr Leavis has imposed on English literature : only odd influences such as Tenniel's on Levine, or odd developments with a by-effect in caricature such as Lavater's rules of physiognomy or the popularizing of silhouettes. Neither is there a distinctive thread which, like the air-twist of a glass cane, the lettering in Brighton rock or the poison vein of the lamprey, runs from beginning to end. Even the motifs of the tattooist have been governed by international conventions more rigorous. For the essence of caricature is the expression of individuality : the subject's, the artist's. It does not disappoint those who scan it for the wellsprings of humour and the mechanics of hilarity, the Freudian arcana of the seaside postcard and the archaeology of the dirty joke. At the same time, its irrepudiable practical objects—to satirize and to entertain—have protected it from the more corrosive humours and nonsenses of modern art movements. Fine art and applied art in one, it has its own humour and nonsense well under control.

'The Incredible Hulk' : cover by **Trimpe** for an American comic, 1969

'The pen is mightier than the sword': caricature of the caricaturist by Trier, Amsterdam

Acknowledgements

The author is extremely grateful to all who lent caricatures and cartoons, or photographs, or gave copyright permissions. His greatest debt is to John Naimaster and Peyton Skipwith of the Fine Art Society, Ltd, who saved him an immense amount of time and trouble in obtaining permissions, and who generously supplied so many excellent photographs. Mrs. Sven Gahlin kindly lent the silhouette caricature alphabet used on the cover.

The author also wishes to thank his father, J. R. Hillier, who read the book in manuscript; Nicholas Orme, who read the proofs; and Philip Mansergh for the loan of a Gillray which, alas, could not be illustrated because of pressure on space. In compensation and in friendship, this book is dedicated to Philip, his wife Yvonne and their daughter Natasha.

157

Index of Artists

159

STUDIO VISTA | DUTTON PICTUREBACKS

edited by David Herbert

British churches by Edwin Smith and Olive Cook
European domestic architecture by Sherban Cantacuzino
Great modern architecture by Sherban Cantacuzino
Modern churches of the world by Robert Maguire and Keith Murray
Modern houses of the world by Sherban Cantacuzino

African sculpture by William Fagg and Margaret Plass
European sculpture by David Bindman
Florentine sculpture by Anthony Bertram
Greek sculpture by John Barron
Indian sculpture by Philip Rawson
Michelangelo by Anthony Bertram
Modern sculpture by Alan Bowness

Art deco by Bevis Hillier
Art nouveau by Mario Amaya
The Bauhaus by Gillian Naylor
Cartoons and caricatures by Bevis Hillier
Dada by Kenneth Coutts-Smith
De Stijl by Paul Overy
Modern graphics by Keith Murgatroyd
Modern prints by Pat Gilmour
Pop art: object and image by Christopher Finch
The Pre-Raphaelites by John Nicoll
Surrealism by Roger Cardinal and Robert Stuart Short
1000 years of drawing by Anthony Bertram

Arms and armour by Howard L. Blackmore
The art of the garden by Miles Hadfield
Art in silver and gold by Gerald Taylor
Costume in pictures by Phillis Cunnington
Firearms by Howard L. Blackmore
Jewelry by Graham Hughes
Modern ballet by John Percival
Modern ceramics by Geoffrey Beard
Modern furniture by Ella Moody
Modern glass by Geoffrey Beard
Motoring history by L. T. C. Rolt
Railway history by C. Hamilton Ellis
Toys by Patrick Murray

Charlie Chaplin: early comedies by Isabel Quigly
The films of Alfred Hitchcock by George Perry
French film by Roy Armes
The great funnies by David Robinson
Greta Garbo by Raymond Durgnat and John Kobal
Marlene Dietrich by John Kobal
Movie monsters by Denis Gifford
New cinema in Britain by Roger Manvell
New cinema in Europe by Roger Manvell
New cinema in the USA by Roger Manvell
The silent cinema by Liam O'Leary